Jigsaw Politics

*Shaping the House
After the 1990 Census*

Jigsaw Politics

*Shaping the House
After the 1990 Census*

Congressional Quarterly Inc.

Congressional Quarterly Inc.

Congressional Quarterly Inc., an editorial research service and publishing company, serves clients in the fields of news, education, business, and government. It combines Congressional Quarterly's specific coverage of Congress, government, and politics with the more general subject range of an affiliated service, Editorial Research Reports.

Congressional Quarterly publishes the *Congressional Quarterly Weekly Report* and a variety of books, including college political science textbooks under the CQ Press imprint and public affairs paperbacks on developing issues and events. CQ also publishes information directories and reference books on the federal government, national elections, and politics, including the *Guide to the Presidency,* the *Guide to Congress,* the *Guide to the U.S. Supreme Court,* the *Guide to U.S. Elections, Politics in America,* and *Congress A to Z: CQ's Ready Reference Encyclopedia.* The *CQ Almanac,* a compendium of legislation for one session of Congress, is published each year. *Congress and the Nation,* a record of government for a presidential term, is published every four years.

CQ publishes the *Congressional Monitor,* a daily report on current and future activities of congressional committees, and several newsletters including *Congressional Insight,* a weekly analysis of congressional action, and *Campaign Practices Reports,* a semimonthly update on campaign laws.

An electronic online information system, Washington Alert, provides immediate access to CQ's databases of legislative action, votes, schedules, profiles, and analyses.

Copyright © 1990 Congressional Quarterly Inc.
1414 22nd Street, N.W.
Washington, D.C. 20037

Printed in the United States of America

Library of Congress Cataloging-in-Publication Data

Jigsaw politics: shaping the House after the 1990 Census.
    p. cm.
  ISBN 0-87187-576-4:
    1. United States. Congress. House--Election districts.
  2. United States--Census, 21st, 1990. 3. Apportionment (Election
  law)--United States--History. I. Congressional Quarterly, inc.
  JK1341.J54 1990
  328.73' 07345--dc20
                                                              90-34907
                                                                  CIP

Major Contributor: Robert Benenson
Other Contributors: Peter Bragdon, Rhodes Cook, Phil Duncan, Kenneth E. Jaques
Editor: Carolyn Goldinger
Indexer: Bernice Eisen
Cover Design: Dan Royer

Congressional Quarterly Inc.

Andrew Barnes   *Chairman*
Richard R. Edmonds   *President*
Neil Skene   *Editor and Publisher*
Robert W. Merry   *Executive Editor*
John J. Coyle   *Associate Publisher*
Michael L. Koempel   *Director, Information Services*
Robert E. Cuthriell   *Director, Development*

Book Division

Patrick Bernuth   *General Manager, Book Division*

Book Editorial

David R. Tarr   *Director, Book Department*
Nancy A. Lammers   *Managing Editor*
Carolyn Goldinger   *Senior Editor*
Margaret Seawell Benjaminson   *Developmental Editor*
Ann Davies   *Project Editor*
Colleen McGuiness   *Project Editor*
Jamie R. Holland   *Production Editor*
Nancy Kervin   *Production Editor*
Ann F. O'Malley   *Production Editor*
Jerry Orvedahl   *Production Editor*
Linda White   *Administrative Assistant*

Book Marketing

Kathryn C. Suárez   *Director, Book Marketing*
Jacqueline A. Davey   *Library Marketing Manager*
Kimberly B. Hatton   *Marketing Coordinator*
Leslie Brenowitz   *Administrative Assistant*

Production

I. D. Fuller   *Production Manager*
Michael Emanuel   *Assistant Production Manager*
Jhonnie G. Bailey   *Assistant to the Production Manager*

Contents

Part I

Reapportionment
and
Redistricting

1

Background and Process

Reapportionment is the redistribution of the 435 seats in the U.S. House of Representatives among the states to reflect shifts in population; redistricting is the redrawing of congressional district lines within each state. They are among the most important processes in the U.S. political system. They help determine whether the House will be dominated by Democrats or Republicans, liberals or conservatives, and whether racial or ethnic minorities receive fair representation.

Reapportionment and redistricting occur every ten years on the basis of the decennial population census. States whose populations grew quickly over the previous ten years gain congressional seats, while those that lost population or grew much more slowly than the national average lose seats. The number of House delegates for the rest of the states remains the same.

The states that gain or lose seats must make extensive changes in their congressional maps. Even those states with stable delegations must make modifications that account for population shifts within their boundaries in accordance with Supreme Court "one-person, one-vote" rulings.

Despite their importance to the political process, reapportionment and redistricting draw little interest from the general public. This lack of attention is ironic, wrote Andrea J. Wollock in the January 1982 issue of *State Legislatures,* because reapportionment is not only a "supremely important" political issue but also "a source of unsurpassed political drama and intrigue." Partisan interests are enhanced; personal ambitions of powerful politicians are furthered. Incumbents are protected or politically crippled. Tempers flare and fists fly, as they did during a redistricting debate in the Illinois Legislature in 1981.

Among the many unique features to emerge in the remarkable nation-creating endeavor of 1787 was a national legislative body whose membership was to be elected by the people and apportioned on the basis of population. In keeping with the nature of the Constitution, however, only fundamental rules and regulations were provided. How to interpret and implement the instructions contained in the document were left to future generations.

Within this flexible framework, many questions soon arose concerning the House of Representatives. How large was it to be? What mathematical formula was to be used in calculating the distribution of seats among the various states? Were the representatives to be elected at large or by districts? If by districts, what standards should be used in fixing their boundaries? Congress and the courts have been wrestling with these questions for almost two hundred years.

Until the mid-twentieth century, such questions generally remained in the hands of the legislators. But with growing concentration of the population in urban areas, variations in population among congressional districts became more pronounced. Efforts to persuade Congress to redress the grievance of heavily populated but under-represented areas proved unsuccessful. Rural legislators were so intent on preventing power from slipping out of their control that they managed to block reapportionment of the House following the census of 1920.

Not long afterward, litigants tried to persuade the Supreme Court to order the states to revise congressional district boundaries in line with population shifts. After initial failure, a breakthrough occurred in 1964 in the case of *Wesberry v. Sanders.* The Court declared that the Constitution required that "as nearly as practicable, one man's vote in a congressional election is to be worth as much as another's."

In the years that followed the Court repeatedly reaffirmed its "one person, one vote" requirement. In *Karcher v. Daggett* in 1983 the Court held that no deviation from that principle was permissible unless the state proved that the population variation was necessary to achieve some legitimate goal. This ruling immediately drew fire from those who thought it would allow states to ignore several other traditional factors involved in redistricting—such as compactness of the district or integrity of county and city lines—in their quest for districts of precisely equal populations.

Early History

Modern legislative bodies are descended from the councils of feudal lords and gentry that medieval kings summoned for the purpose of raising revenues and armies. These councils did not represent a king's subjects in any modern sense. They represented certain groups of subjects, such as the nobility, the clergy, the landed gentry, and town merchants. Representation was by interest groups and bore no relation to equal representation for equal numbers of people. In England the king's council became Parliament, with the higher nobility and clergy making up the House of Lords and representatives of the gentry and merchants making up the House of Commons.

Beginning as little more than administrative and advisory arms of the throne, royal councils in time developed into law-making bodies and acquired powers that eventually eclipsed those of the monarchs they served. The power struggle in England climaxed during the Cromwellian period when the king was executed and a "benevolent" dictatorship was set up under Oliver Cromwell. By 1800 Parliament was clearly the superior branch of government.

During the eighteenth and early nineteenth centuries, as the power of Parliament grew, the English became increasingly concerned about the "representativeness" of their system of apportionment. Newly developing industrial cities had no more representation in the House of Commons than small, almost-deserted country towns. Small constituencies were bought and sold. Men from these empty "rotten boroughs" often were sent to Parliament representing a single "patron" landowner or clique of wealthy men. It was not until the Reform Act of 1832 that Parliament curbed such excesses and turned toward a representative system based on population.

The growth of the powers of Parliament, as well as the development of English ideas of representation during the seventeenth and eighteenth centuries, had a profound effect on the colonists in America. Representative assemblies were unifying forces behind the breakaway of the colonies from England and the establishment of the newly independent country.

Colonists in America, generally modeling their legislatures after England's, used both population and land units as bases for apportionment. Patterns of early representation varied. "Nowhere did representation bear any uniform relation to the number of electors. Here and there the factor of size had been crudely recognized," Robert Luce pointed out in his book *Legislative Principles*.

In New England the town usually was the basis for representation. In the Middle Atlantic region the county frequently was used. Virginia used the county with additional representation for specified cities. In many areas, towns and counties were fairly equal in population, and territorial representation afforded roughly equal representation for equal numbers of people. Delaware's three counties, for example, were of almost equal population and had the same representation in the Legislature. But in Virginia the disparity was enormous (from 951 people in one county to 22,015 in another). Thomas Jefferson criticized the state's constitution on the ground that "among those who share the representation, the shares are unequal."

The Continental Congress, with representation from every colony, proclaimed in the Declaration of Independence in 1776 that governments derive "their just powers from the consent of the governed" and that "the right of representation in the legislature" is an "inestimable right" of the people. The Constitutional Convention of 1787 included representatives from all the states. However, in neither of these bodies were the state delegations or voting powers proportional to population.

Andrew Hacker, in his book *Congressional Districting*, said that to understand what the Framers of the Constitution had in mind when they drew up the section con-

cerning the House of Representatives, it was necessary to study closely several sources: the Constitution itself, the recorded discussions and debates at the Constitutional Convention, *The Federalist Papers* (essays written by Alexander Hamilton, John Jay, and James Madison in defense of the Constitution), and the deliberations of the states' ratifying conventions.

The Constitution declares only that each state is to be allotted a certain number of representatives. It does not state specifically that congressional districts must be equal or nearly equal in population. Nor does it require specifically that a state create districts at all. However, it seems clear that the first clause of Article I, Section 2, providing that House members should be chosen "by the people of the several states," indicated that the House of Representatives, in contrast to the Senate, was to represent people rather than states. "It follows," Hacker wrote, "that if the states are to have equal representation in the upper chamber, then individuals are to be equally represented in the lower body."

The third clause of Article I, Section 2, provided that congressional apportionment among the states must be according to population. But Hacker argued,

> there is little point in giving the states congressmen "according to their respective numbers" if the states do not redistribute the members of their delegations on the same principle. For representatives are not the property of the states, as are the senators, but rather belong to the people who happen to reside within the boundaries of those states. Thus, each citizen has a claim to be regarded as a political unit equal in value to his neighbors.

In this and similar ways, constitutional scholars have argued the case for single-member congressional districts deduced from the wording of the Constitution itself.

The issue of unequal representation

arose only once during debate in the Constitutional Convention. The occasion was Madison's defense of Article I, Section 4, of the proposed Constitution, giving Congress the power to override state regulations on "the times ... and manner" of holding elections for members of Congress. Madison's argument related to the fact that many state legislatures of the time were badly malapportioned: "The inequality of the representation in the legislatures of particular states would produce a like inequality in their representation in the national legislature, as it was presumable that the counties having the power in the former case would secure it to themselves in the latter."

The implication was that states would create congressional districts and that unequal districting was undesirable and should be prevented.

Madison made this interpretation even more clear in his contributions to *The Federalist Papers*. Arguing in favor of the relatively small size of the projected House of Representatives, he wrote in *No. 56:* "Divide the largest state into ten or twelve districts and it will be found that there will be no peculiar local interests ... which will not be within the knowledge of the Representative of the district."

In the same paper Madison said, "The Representatives of each state will not only bring with them a considerable knowledge of its laws, and a local knowledge of their respective districts, but will probably in all cases have been members, and may even at the very time be members, of the state legislature, where all the local information and interests of the state are assembled, and from whence they may easily be conveyed by a very few hands into the legislature of the United States." And, finally, in *Federalist Paper No. 57* Madison stated that "each Representative of the United States will be elected by five or six thousand citizens." In making these arguments, Madison seems to have assumed that all or most representatives would be elected by districts rather than at large.

In the states' ratifying conventions, the grant to Congress by Article I, Section 4, of ultimate jurisdiction over the "times, places and manner of holding elections" (except the places of choosing senators) held the attention of many delegates. There were differences over the merits of this section, but no justification of unequal districts was prominently used to attack the grant of power. Further evidence that individual districts were the intention of the Founding Fathers was given in the New York ratifying convention, when Alexander Hamilton said, "The natural and proper mode of holding elections will be to divide the state into districts in proportion to the number to be elected. This state will consequently be divided at first into six."

From his study of the sources relating to the question of congressional districting, Hacker concluded,

> There is, then, a good deal of evidence that those who framed and ratified the Constitution intended that the House of Representatives have as its constituency a public in which the votes of all citizens were of equal weight.... The House of Representatives was designed to be a popular chamber, giving the same electoral power to all who had the vote. And the concern of Madison ... that districts be equal in size was an institutional step in the direction of securing this democratic principle.

Reapportionment of Seats

Article I, Section 2, Clause 3, of the Constitution laid down the basic rules for apportionment and reapportionment of seats in the House of Representatives:

> Representatives ... shall be apportioned among the several States which may be

included within this Union, according to their respective Numbers, which shall be determined by adding to the whole Number of free Persons, including those Bound to Service for a Term of Years, and excluding Indians not taxed, three-fifths of all other Persons. The actual Enumeration shall be made within three Years after the first Meeting of the Congress of the United States, and within every subsequent Term of Ten years, in such manner as they shall by Law direct. The number of Representatives shall not exceed one for every thirty Thousand, but each State shall have at Least one Representative.

The Constitution made the first apportionment, which was to remain in effect until the first census was taken. No reliable figures on the population were available at the time. The thirteen states were allocated the following numbers of representatives: New Hampshire, three; Massachusetts, eight; Rhode Island and Providence Plantations, one; Connecticut, five; New York, six; New Jersey, four; Pennsylvania, eight; Delaware, one; Maryland, six; Virginia, ten; North Carolina, five; South Carolina, five; and Georgia, three. The apportionment of seats—sixty-five in all—thus mandated by the Constitution remained in effect during the First and Second Congresses (1789-1793).

Apparently realizing that apportionment of the House was likely to become a major bone of contention, the First Congress submitted to the states a proposed constitutional amendment containing a formula to be used in future reapportionments. The amendment, which was not ratified, provided that following the taking of a decennial census there would be one representative for every 30,000 persons until the House membership reached 100, "after which the proportion shall be so regulated by Congress that there shall be not less than 100 representatives, nor less than one representative for every 40,000 persons, until the number of representatives shall amount to

200, after which the proportion shall be so regulated by Congress, that there shall not be less than 200 representatives, nor more than one representative for every 50,000 persons."

First Apportionment by Congress

The states' refusal to ratify the reapportionment-formula amendment forced Congress to enact apportionment legislation after the first census was taken in 1790. The first apportionment bill was sent to the president on March 23, 1792. Washington sent the bill back to Congress without his signature—the first presidential veto.

The bill had incorporated the constitutional minimum of 30,000 as the size of each district. But the population of each state was not a simple multiple of 30,000. Significant fractions were left over when the number of people in each state was divided by 30,000. For example, Vermont was found to be entitled to 2.851 representatives, New Jersey to 5.98, and Virginia to 21.018. A formula had to be found that would deal in the fairest possible manner with unavoidable variations from exact equality.

Accordingly, Congress proposed in the first apportionment bill to distribute the members on a fixed ratio of one representative for each 30,000 inhabitants, and give an additional member to each state with a fraction exceeding one-half. Washington's veto was based on the belief that eight states would receive more than one representative for each 30,000 persons under this formula.

A motion to override the veto was unsuccessful. A new bill meeting the president's objections was introduced April 9, 1792, and approved April 14. The act provided for a ratio of one member for every 33,000 inhabitants and fixed the exact number of representatives to which each state was entitled. The total membership of the

House was to be 105. In dividing the population of the various states by 33,000, all remainders were to be disregarded. Thomas Jefferson devised the solution, known as the method of rejected fractions.

Jefferson's Method

Jefferson's method of reapportionment resulted in great inequalities among districts. A Vermont district would contain 42,766 inhabitants, a New Jersey district 35,911, and a Virginia district only 33,187. Emphasis was placed on what was considered the ideal size of a congressional district rather than on what the size of the House ought to be. This method was in use until 1840.

The reapportionment act based on the census of 1800 continued the ratio of 33,000, which provided a House of 141 members. Debate on the third apportionment bill began in the House on November 22, 1811, and the bill was sent to the president on December 21. The ratio was fixed at 35,000, yielding a House of 181 members. Following the 1820 census, Congress approved an apportionment bill providing a ratio of 40,000 inhabitants per district. The sum of the quotas for the various states produced a House of 213 members.

The act of May 22, 1832, fixed the ratio at 47,700, resulting in a House of 240 members. Dissatisfaction with the method in use continued, and Daniel Webster launched a vigorous attack against it. He urged adoption of a method that would assign an additional representative to each state with a large fraction. His approach to the reapportionment process was outlined in a report he submitted to Congress in 1832:

> The Constitution, therefore, must be understood not as enjoining an absolute relative equality—because that would be demanding an impossibility—but as requiring of Congress to make the apportionment of Representatives among the several states according to their respective numbers, *as near as may be*. That which cannot be done perfectly must be done in a manner as near perfection as can be.... In such a case approximation becomes a rule.

Following the 1840 census, Congress adopted a reapportionment method similar to that advocated by Webster. The method fixed a ratio of one representative for every 70,680 persons. This figure was reached by deciding on a fixed size of the House in advance (223), dividing that figure into the total national "representative population" and using the result (70,680) as the fixed ratio. The population of each state was then divided by this ratio to find the number of its representatives and the states were assigned an additional representative for each fraction over one-half. Under this method the actual size of the House dropped. *(Congressional apportionment, p. 10)*

The modified reapportionment formula adopted by Congress in 1842 was found to be more satisfactory than the previous method, but another change was made following the census of 1850. The new system was proposed by Rep. Samuel F. Vinton of Ohio and became known as the Vinton method.

Vinton Apportionment Formula

Under the Vinton formula, Congress first fixed the size of the House and then distributed the seats. The total qualifying population of the country was divided by the desired number of representatives, and the resulting number became the ratio of population to each representative. The population of each state was divided by this ratio, and each state received the number of representatives equal to the whole number in the quotient for that state. Then, to reach the required size of the House, additional representatives were assigned based on the remaining fractions, beginning with the state having the largest fraction. This procedure differed from the 1842 method only in the last step, which assigned one representative to every state having a fraction larger than one-half.

Proponents of the Vinton method pointed out that it had the distinct advantage of making it possible to fix the size of the House in advance and to take into account at least the largest fractions. The concern of the House turned from the ideal size of a congressional district to the ideal size of the House itself.

Under the 1842 reapportionment formula, the exact size of the House could not be fixed in advance. If every state with a fraction over one-half were given an additional representative, the House might wind up with a few more or a few less than the desired number. However, under the Vinton method, only states with the largest fractions were given additional House members and only up to the desired total size of the House.

Vinton Apportionments

Six reapportionments were carried out under the Vinton method. The 1850 census act contained three provisions not included in any previous law. First, it required reapportionment not only after the census of 1850 but also after all the subsequent censuses; second, it purported to fix the size of the House permanently at 233 members; and third, it provided in advance for an automatic apportionment by the secretary of the interior under the method prescribed in the act.

Following the census of 1860, according to the provisions of the act passed a decade before, an automatic reapportionment was to be carried out by the Interior Department. However, because the size of the House was to remain at the 1850 level, some states faced loss of representation and

others would gain less than they expected. To avert that possibility, an act was approved March 4, 1862, increasing the size of the House to 241 and giving an extra representative to eight states—Illinois, Iowa, Kentucky, Minnesota, Ohio, Pennsylvania, Rhode Island, and Vermont.

Apportionment legislation following the 1870 census contained several new provisions. The act of February 2, 1872, fixed the size of the House at 283, with the proviso that the number should be increased if new states were admitted. A supplemental act of May 30, 1872, assigned one additional representative each to Alabama, Florida, Indiana, Louisiana, New Hampshire, New York, Pennsylvania, Tennessee, and Vermont.

Another section of the 1872 act provided that no state should thereafter be admitted "without having the necessary population to entitle it to at least one representative fixed by this bill." That provision was found to be unenforceable because no Congress can bind a succeeding Congress. Moreover, no ratio was fixed by the act, although the basis on which the representatives were assigned was 131,425. In 1890 Idaho was admitted with a population of 84,385 and Wyoming with a population of 60,705.

With the Reconstruction era at its height in the South, the reapportionment legislation of 1872 reflected the desire of Congress to enforce Section 2 of the new Fourteenth Amendment. That section attempted to protect the right of blacks to vote by providing for reduction of representation in the House of a state that interfered with the exercise of that right. The number of representatives of such a state was to be reduced in proportion to the number of inhabitants of voting age whose right to go to the polls was denied or abridged. The reapportionment bill repeated the language of the section, but it never was put into

Congressional Apportionment, 1789-1980

Year of Census[1]

	1789†	1790	1800	1810	1820	1830	1840	1850	1860	1870	1880	1890	1900	1910	1930#	1940	1950	1960	1970	1980
Alabama				1*	3	5	7	7	6	8	8	9	9	10	9	9	9	8	7	7
Alaska																	1*	1	1	1
Arizona														1*	1	2	2	3	4	5
Arkansas						1*	1	2	3	4	5	6	7	7	7	7	6	4	4	4
California								2*	3	4	6	7	8	11	20	23	30	38	43	45
Colorado										1*	1	2	3	4	4	4	4	4	5	6
Connecticut	5	7	7	7	6	6	4	4	4	4	4	4	5	5	6	6	6	6	6	6
Delaware	1	1	1	2	1	1	1	1	1	1	1	1	1	1	1	1	1	1	1	1
Florida							1*	1	1	2	2	2	3	4	5	6	8	12	15	19
Georgia	3	2	4	6	7	9	8	8	7	9	10	11	11	12	10	10	10	10	10	10
Hawaii																	1*	2	2	2
Idaho											1*	1	1	2	2	2	2	2	2	2
Illinois				1*	1	3	7	9	14	19	20	22	25	27	27	26	25	24	24	22
Indiana				1*	3	7	10	11	11	13	13	13	13	13	12	11	11	11	11	10
Iowa							2*	2	6	9	11	11	11	11	9	8	8	7	6	6
Kansas									1*	3	7	8	8	8	7	6	6	5	5	5
Kentucky		2	6	10	12	13	10	10	9	10	11	11	11	11	9	9	8	7	7	7
Louisiana				1*	3	3	4	4	5	6	6	6	7	8	8	8	8	8	8	8
Maine				7*	7	8	7	6	5	5	4	4	4	4	3	3	3	2	2	2
Maryland	6	8	9	9	9	8	6	6	5	6	6	6	6	6	6	6	7	8	8	8
Massachusetts	8	14	17	13‡	13	12	10	11	10	11	12	13	14	16	15	14	14	12	12	11
Michigan						1*	3	4	6	9	11	12	12	13	17	17	18	19	19	18
Minnesota								2*	2	3	5	7	9	10	9	9	9	8	8	8
Mississippi				1*	1	2	4	5	5	6	7	7	8	8	7	7	6	5	5	5
Missouri					1*	2	5	7	9	13	14	15	16	16	13	13	11	10	10	9

State	1789	1790	1800	1810	1820	1830	1840	1850	1860	1870	1880	1890	1900	1910	1930	1940	1950	1960	1970	1980
Montana											1*	1	1	2	2	2	2	2	2	2
Nebraska									1*	1	3	6	6	6	5	4	4	3	3	3
Nevada									1*	1	1	1	1	1	1	1	1	1	1	2
New Hampshire	3	4	5	6	6	5	4	3	3	3	2	2	2	2	2	2	2	2	2	2
New Jersey	4	5	6	6	6	6	5	5	5	7	7	8	10	12	14	14	14	15	15	14
New Mexico														1*	1	2	2	2	2	3
New York	6	10	17	27	34	40	34	33	31	33	34	34	37	43	45	45	43	41	39	34
North Carolina	5	10	12	13	13	13	9	8	7	8	9	9	10	10	11	12	12	11	11	11
North Dakota											1*	1	2	3	2	2	2	2	1	1
Ohio			1*	6	14	19	21	21	19	20	21	21	21	22	24	23	23	24	23	21
Oklahoma													5*	8	9	8	6	6	6	6
Oregon								1*	1	1	1	2	2	3	3	4	4	4	4	5
Pennsylvania	8	13	18	23	26	28	24	25	24	27	28	30	32	36	34	33	30	27	25	23
Rhode Island	1	2	2	2	2	2	2	2	2	2	2	2	2	3	2	2	2	2	2	2
South Carolina	5	6	8	9	9	9	7	6	4	5	7	7	7	7	6	6	6	6	6	6
South Dakota											2*	2	2	3	2	2	2	2	2	1
Tennessee		1*	3	6	9	13	11	10	8	10	10	10	10	10	9	10	9	9	8	9
Texas							2*	2	4	6	11	13	16	18	21	21	22	23	24	27
Utah												1*	1	2	2	2	2	2	2	3
Vermont		2	4	6	5	5	4	3	3	3	2	2	2	2	1	1	1	1	1	1
Virginia	10	19	22	23	22	21	15	13	11	9	10	10	10	10	9	9	10	10	10	10
Washington											1*	2	3	5	6	6	7	7	7	8
West Virginia									3*	3	4	4	5	6	6	6	6	5	4	4
Wisconsin							2*	3	6	8	9	10	11	11	10	10	10	10	9	9
Wyoming											1*	1	1	1	1	1	1	1	1	1
Total	65	106	142	186	213	242	232	237	243	293	332	357	391	435	435	435	435	437**	435	435

[1] Apportionment effective with congressional election two years after census.

† Constitution ratified. Original apportionment made in Constitution, pending first census.

No apportionment was made in 1920.

* These figures are not based on any census, but indicate the provisional representation accorded newly admitted states by the Congress, pending the next census.

‡ Twenty members were assigned to Massachusetts, but seven of these were credited to Maine when that area became a state.

** Normally 435, but temporarily increased two seats by Congress when Alaska and Hawaii became states.

Source: *Biographical Directory of the American Congress* and Bureau of the Census

effect because of the difficulty of determining the exact number of people whose right to vote was being abridged.

The reapportionment act of February 25, 1882, provided for a House of 325 members, with additional members for any new states admitted to the Union. No new apportionment provisions were added. The acts of February 7, 1891, and January 16, 1901, were routine as far as apportionment was concerned. The 1891 measure provided for a House of 356 members, and the 1901 statute increased the number to 386.

Despite the apparent advantages of the Vinton method, certain difficulties revealed themselves as the formula was applied. Zechariah Chafee, Jr., of the Harvard Law School summarized these problems in an article in the *Harvard Law Review* in 1929. The method, he pointed out, suffered from what he called the "Alabama paradox." Under that aberration, an increase in the total size of the House might be accompanied by an actual loss of a seat by some states, even though there had been no corresponding change in population. This phenomenon first appeared in tables prepared for Congress in 1881, which gave Alabama eight members in a House of 299 but only seven members in a House of 300. It could even happen that the state that lost a seat was the one state that had expanded in population, while all the others had fewer people.

Chafee concluded from his study of the Vinton method:

> Thus, it is unsatisfactory to fix the ratio of population per Representative before seats are distributed. Either the size of the House comes out haphazard, or, if this be determined in advance, the absurdities of the "Alabama paradox" vitiate the apportionment. Under present conditions, it is essential to determine the size of the House in advance; the problem thereafter is to distribute the required number of seats among the several states as nearly as

possible in proportion to their respective populations so that no state is treated unfairly in comparison with any other state.

Maximum Membership of House

On August 8, 1911, the membership of the House was fixed at 433. Provision was made in the reapportionment act of that date for the addition of one representative each from Arizona and New Mexico, which were expected to become states in the near future. Thus, the size of the House reached 435, where it has remained up to the present with the exception of a brief period (1959-1963) when the admission of Alaska and Hawaii raised the total temporarily to 437.

Limiting the size of the House amounted to recognition that the body soon would expand to unmanageable proportions if Congress continued the practice of adding new seats every ten years to match population gains without depriving any state of its existing representation. Agreement on a fixed number made the task of reapportionment all the more difficult when the population not only increased but became much more mobile. Population shifts brought Congress up hard against the politically painful necessity of taking seats away from slow-growing states to give the fast-growing states adequate representation.

A new mathematical calculation was adopted for the reapportionment following the 1910 census. Devised by W. F. Willcox of Cornell University, the new system established a priority list that assigned seats progressively, beginning with the first seat above the constitutional minimum of at least one seat for each state. When there were forty-eight states, this method was used to assign the forty-ninth member, the fiftieth member, and so on, until the agreed upon size of the House was reached. The method was called major fractions and was used after the censuses of 1910, 1930, and 1940. There was no reapportionment after the 1920 census.

1920s Struggle

The results of the fourteenth decennial census were announced December 17, 1920, just after the short session of the 66th Congress convened. The 1920 census showed that for the first time in history most Americans were urban residents. This came as a profound shock to people accustomed to emphasizing the nation's rural traditions and the virtues of life on farms and in small towns. Rural legislators immediately mounted an attack on the census results and succeeded in postponing reapportionment legislation for almost a decade.

Thomas Jefferson once wrote:

Those who labor in the earth are the chosen people of God, if ever He had a chosen people, whose breasts He had made His peculiar deposit for substantial and genuine virtue.... The mobs of great cities add just as much to the support of pure government as sores do to the strength of the human body.... I think our governments will remain virtuous for many centuries as long as they are chiefly agricultural: and this shall be as long as there shall be vacant lands in any part of America. When they get piled up upon one another in large cities as in Europe, they will become corrupt as in Europe.

As their power waned throughout the latter part of the nineteenth century and the early part of the twentieth, farmers and their spokesmen clung to the Jeffersonian belief that somehow they were more pure and virtuous than the growing number of urban residents. When finally faced with the fact that they were in the minority, these country residents put up a strong rearguard action to prevent the inevitable shift of congressional districts to the cities.

Rural representatives insisted that, since the 1920 census was taken as of January 1, the farm population had been undercounted. In support of this contention, they argued that many farm laborers were seasonally employed in the cities at that time of year. Furthermore, midwinter road conditions probably had prevented enumerators from visiting many farms, they said; and other farmers were said to have been uncounted because they were absent on winter vacation trips. The change of the census date to January 1 in 1920 had been made to conform to recommendations of the U.S. Department of Agriculture, which had asserted that the census should be taken early in the year if an accurate statistical picture of farming conditions was to be obtained.

Another point raised by rural legislators was that large numbers of unnaturalized aliens were congregated in northern cities, with the result that these cities gained at the expense of constituencies made up mostly of citizens of the United States. Rep. Homer Hoch, R-Kan., submitted a table showing that, in a House of 435 representatives, exclusion from the census count of persons not naturalized would have altered the allocation of seats in sixteen states. Southern and western farming states would have retained the number of seats allocated to them in 1911 or would have gained, while northern industrial states and California would have lost or at least would have gained fewer seats.

A constitutional amendment to exclude all aliens from the enumeration for purposes of reapportionment was proposed during the 70th Congress (1927-1929) by Hoch, Sen. Arthur Capper, R-Kan., and others. During the Senate Commerce Committee's hearings on reapportionment, Sen. Frederick M. Sackett, R-Ky., and Sen. Lawrence D. Tyson, D-Tenn., said they too intended to propose amendments to the same effect. But nothing further came of the proposals.

Reapportionment Bills Opposed

The first bill to reapportion the House according to the 1920 census was drafted by the House Census Committee early in 1921. Proceeding on the principle that no state should have its representation reduced, the committee proposed to increase the total number of representatives from 435 to 483. But the House voted 267-76 to keep its membership at 435 and passed the bill so amended on January 19, 1921. Eleven states would have lost seats and eight would have gained. The bill then was blocked by a Senate committee, where it died when the 66th Congress expired March 4, 1921.

Early in the 67th Congress, the House Census Committee again reported a bill, this time fixing the total membership at 460, an increase of 25. Two states—Maine and Massachusetts—would have lost one representative each and sixteen states would have gained. On the House floor an unsuccessful attempt was made to fix the number at the existing 435, and the House sent the bill back to committee.

During the 68th Congress (1923-1925), the House Census Committee failed to report any reapportionment bill, and midway in the 69th Congress (1925-1927) it became apparent that the committee would not produce a reapportionment measure. Accordingly, on April 8, 1926, Rep. Henry E. Barbour, R-Calif., moved that the committee be discharged from further consideration of a bill identical with that passed by the House in 1921 keeping the chamber's membership at 435.

Chairman Bertrand H. Snell, N.Y., of the House Rules Committee, representing the Republican leadership of the House, raised a point of order against Barbour's motion. The Speaker of the House, Nicholas Longworth, R-Ohio, pointed out that decisions of earlier Speakers tended to indicate that reapportionment had been considered a matter of "constitutional privilege" and that Barbour's motion must be held in order if these precedents were followed. But the Speaker said he doubted whether the precedents had been interpreted correctly. He therefore submitted to the House the question of whether the pending motion should be considered privileged. The House sustained the Rules Committee by voting 87-265 not to consider the question privileged.

Intervention by Coolidge

President Calvin Coolidge, who previously had made no reference to reapportionment in his communications to Congress, announced in January 1927 that he favored passage of a new apportionment bill during the short session of the 69th Congress, which would end in less than two months. The House Census Committee refused to act. Its chairman, Rep. E. Hart Fenn, R-Conn., therefore moved in the House on March 2, 1927, to suspend the rules and pass a bill he had introduced authorizing the secretary of commerce to reapportion the House immediately after the 1930 census. The motion was voted down 183-197.

The Fenn bill was rewritten early in the 70th Congress (1927-1929) to give Congress itself a chance to act before the proposed reapportionment by the secretary of commerce should go into effect. The bill was submitted to the House, which, on May 18, 1928, voted 186-165 to recommit it to the Census Committee. After minor changes, the Fenn bill was again reported to the House and was passed on January 11, 1929. No record vote was taken on passage of the bill, but a motion to return it to the committee was rejected 134-227.

Four days later, the reapportionment bill was reported by the Senate Commerce Committee. Repeated efforts to bring it up for floor action ahead of other bills failed. Its supporters gave up the fight on February 27, 1929—five days before the end of the session, when it became evident that senators from states slated to lose representation were ready to carry on a filibuster that would have blocked not only reapportionment but all other measures.

Intervention by Hoover

As the date of the next census became imminent, President Herbert Hoover listed provision for the 1930 census and reapportionment as "matters of emergency legislation" that should be acted upon in the special session of the 71st Congress, which was convened on April 15, 1929. In response to this urgent request, the Senate June 13 passed, 48-37, a combined census-reapportionment bill that had been approved by voice vote of the House two days earlier.

The 1929 law established a permanent system of reapportioning the 435 House seats following each census. It provided that immediately after the convening of the 71st Congress for its short session in December 1930, the president was to transmit to Congress a statement showing the population of each state together with an apportionment of representatives to each state based on the existing size of the House. Failing enactment of new apportionment legislation, that apportionment would go into effect without further action and would remain in effect for ensuing elections to the House of Representatives until another census had been taken and another reapportionment made.

Because two decades had passed between reapportionments, a greater shift than usual took place following the 1930 census. California's House delegation was almost doubled, rising from eleven to twenty. Michigan gained four seats, Texas three, and New Jersey, New York, and Ohio two each. Twenty-one states lost a total of twenty-seven seats; Missouri lost three, and Georgia, Iowa, Kentucky, and Pennsylvania each lost two.

To test the fairness of two allocation methods—the familiar major fractions and the new equal proportions system—the 1929 act required the president to report the distribution of seats by both methods. But, pending legislation to the contrary, the method of major fractions was to be used.

The two methods gave an identical distribution of seats based on 1930 census figures. However, in 1940 the two methods gave different results: under major fractions, Michigan would have gained a seat lost by Arkansas; under equal proportions, there would have been no change in either state. The automatic reapportionment provisions of the 1929 act went into effect in January 1941. But the House Census Committee moved to reverse the result, favoring the certain Democratic seat in Arkansas over a possible Republican gain if the seat were shifted to Michigan. The Democratic-controlled Congress went along, adopting equal proportions as the method to be used in reapportionment calculations after the 1950 and subsequent censuses, and making this action retroactive to January 1941 to save Arkansas its seat.

While politics doubtless played a part in the timing of the action taken in 1941, the method of equal proportions had come to be accepted as the best available. It had been worked out by Edward V. Huntington of Harvard in 1921. At the request of the Speaker of the House, all known methods of apportionment were considered in 1929 by the National Academy of Sciences Committee on Apportionment. The committee expressed its preference for equal proportions.

Method of Equal Proportions

The method of equal proportions involves complicated mathematical calculations. In brief, each of the fifty states is initially assigned the one seat to which every state is entitled by the Constitution. Then "priority numbers" for states to receive second seats, third seats, and so on are calculated by dividing the state's population by the square root of n(n-1), where "n" is the number of seats for that state. The priority numbers are then lined up in order and the seats given to the states with priority numbers until 435 are awarded.

The method is designed to make the *proportional* difference between the average district size in any two states as small as possible. For instance, using 1980 census figures, if New Mexico got three seats and Indiana got ten, as occurred under the method of equal proportions, New Mexico would have an average district size of 433,323, and Indiana would have an average district size of 549,018. That makes Indiana's average district 27 percent larger than New Mexico's. On the other hand, if New Mexico got two seats and Indiana got eleven, as would have happened if the major fractions method had been used in 1980, New Mexico's average district of 649,984 would be 30 percent larger than Indiana's average of 499,107.

Two respected private statisticians, M. L. Balinski and H. P. Young, have argued that the equal proportions method has "cheated the larger states, and given undue representation to the smaller ones," in violation of the Supreme Court's one-person, one-vote rule. They have advocated a return to the Vinton method of apportionment. Such a bill was introduced in Congress in early 1981, but it received little attention and died at the end of the session.

Redistricting: Drawing the Lines

Although the Constitution contained provisions for the apportionment of U.S. House seats among the states, it was silent about how the members should be elected. From the beginning most states divided their territory into geographic districts, permitting only one member of Congress to be elected from each district.

But some states allowed would-be House members to run at large, with voters able to cast as many votes as there were seats to be filled. Still other states created what were known as multimember districts, in which a single geographic unit would elect two or more members of the House. At various times, some states used combinations of these methods. For example, a state might elect ten representatives from ten individual districts and two at large.

In the first few elections to the House, New Hampshire, Pennsylvania, New Jersey, and Georgia elected their representatives at large, as did Rhode Island and Delaware, the two states with only a single representative. Districts were used in Massachusetts, New York, Maryland, Virginia, and South Carolina. In Connecticut a preliminary election was held to nominate three times as many persons as the number of representatives to be chosen at large in the subsequent election. In 1840, twenty-two of the thirty-one states elected their representatives by districts. New Hampshire, New Jersey, Georgia, Alabama, Mississippi, and Missouri, with a combined representation of thirty-three House seats, elected their representatives at large. Three states, Arkansas, Delaware, and Florida, had only one representative each.

Those states that used congressional districts quickly developed what came to be known as the gerrymander. The term refers to the practice of drawing district lines so as to maximize the advantage of a political party or interest group. The name originated from a salamander-shaped congressional district created by the Massachusetts Legislature in 1812 when Elbridge Gerry was governor. *(Box, p. 17)*

Constant efforts had been made during the early 1800s to lay down national rules, by means of a constitutional amendment,

for congressional districting. The first resolution proposing a mandatory division of
each state into districts was introduced in
Congress in 1800. In 1802 the legislatures
of Vermont and North Carolina adopted
resolutions in support of such action. From
1816 to 1826, twenty-two state resolutions
were adopted proposing the election of representatives by districts.

In Congress, Sen. Mahlon Dickerson,
D-N.J., proposed such an amendment regularly almost every year from 1817 to 1826.
It was adopted by the Senate three times, in
1819, 1820, and 1822, but each time it
failed to reach a vote in the House.

Because most states accepted the principle of local representation, congressional
efforts to pass a constitutional amendment
were unsuccessful. Instead, a law was
passed in 1842 that required contiguous
single-member congressional districts. That
law required representatives to be "elected
by districts composed of contiguous territory equal in number to the representatives
to which said state may be entitled, no one
district electing more than one Representative."

When President John Tyler signed the
bill, he appended to it a memorandum
voicing doubt as to the constitutionality of
the districting provisions. The memorandum precipitated a minor constitutional crisis. The House, urged on by Rep. John
Quincy Adams of Massachusetts, appointed
a select committee to consider the action of
the president. Chaired by the aging former
president, the committee drew up a resolution protesting Tyler's action as "unwarranted by the Constitution and laws of the
United States, injurious to the public interest, and of evil example for the future; and
this House do hereby solemnly protest
against the said act of the President and
against its ever being repeated or adduced
as a precedent hereafter." The House took
no action on the resolution; several attempts

Origins of the Gerrymander

The practice of "gerrymandering"—the excessive manipulation of
the shape of a legislative district to
benefit a certain incumbent or
party—is probably as old as the Re-
public, but the name originated in
1812. In that year the Massachusetts
Legislature carved out of Essex
County a district that historian John
Fiske said had a "dragonlike con-
tour." When the painter Gilbert Stu-
art saw the misshapen district, he
penciled in a head, wings, and claws
and exclaimed: "That will do for a
salamander!"—to which editor Benjamin Russell replied: "Better say a
Gerrymander!"—after Gov. Elbridge
Gerry of Massachusetts.

to call it up under suspension of the rules failed to receive the necessary two-thirds vote.

The districting provisions of the 1842 act were not repeated in the legislation that followed the 1850 census. But in 1862 an act separate from the reapportionment act revived the provisions of the act of 1842 requiring districts to be composed of contiguous territory.

The 1872 reapportionment act again repeated the districting provisions and went even further by adding that districts should contain "as nearly as practicable an equal number of inhabitants." Similar provisions were included in the acts of 1881 and 1891. In the act of January 16, 1901, the words "compact territory" were added, and the clause then read "contiguous and compact territory and containing as nearly as practicable an equal number of inhabitants." This requirement appeared also in the legislation of August 8, 1911. (The "contiguous and compact" provisions of the act subsequently lapsed, and Congress has never replaced them.)

Several unsuccessful attempts were made to enforce redistricting provisions. Despite the districting requirements of the act of June 25, 1842, New Hampshire, Georgia, Mississippi, and Missouri elected their representatives at large that autumn. When the House elected at that time convened for its first session on December 4, 1843, objection was made to seating the representatives of the four states. The dispute was referred to the Committee on Elections. The majority report of the committee, submitted by its chairman, Rep. Stephen A. Douglas, D-Ill., asserted that the act of 1842 was not binding upon the states and that the representatives in question were entitled to their seats. An amendment to the majority report deleted all reference to the apportionment law. A minority report by Rep. Garrett David, Whig-

Ky., contended that the members had not been elected according to the Constitution and the laws and were not entitled to their seats.

The matter was debated in the House February 6-14, 1844. With the Democratic party holding a majority of more than sixty, and with eighteen of the twenty-one challenged members being Democrats, the House decided to seat the members. However, by 1848 all four states had come around to electing their representatives by districts.

The next challenge a House representative encountered over federal districting laws occurred in 1901. A charge was leveled that the existing Kentucky redistricting law did not comply with the redistricting provision of the federal reapportionment law of January 16, 1901; the charge aimed at preventing the seating of Rep. George G. Gilbert, D, of Kentucky's 8th District. The committee assigned to investigate the matter turned aside the challenge, asserting that the federal act was not binding on the states. The reasons given were practical and political:

> Your committee are therefore of opinion that a proper construction of the Constitution does not warrant the conclusion that by that instrument Congress is clothed with power to determine the boundaries of Congressional districts, or to revise the acts of a State Legislature in fixing such boundaries; and your committee is further of opinion that even if such power is to be implied from the language of the Constitution, it would be in the last degree unwise and intolerable that it should exercise it. To do so would be to put into the hands of Congress the ability to disfranchise, in effect, a large body of the electors. It would give Congress the power to apply to all the States, in favor of one party, a general system of gerrymandering. It is true that the same method is to a large degree resorted to by the several states, but the division of political power is so general and diverse that notwithstanding

the inherent vice of the system of gerry-mandering, some kind of equality of distribution results.

In 1908 the Virginia Legislature transferred Floyd County from the 5th District to the 6th District. As a result, the population of the 5th was reduced from 175,579 to 160,191 and that of the 6th was increased from 181,571 to 196,959. The average for the state was 185,418. When the newly elected representative from the 5th District, Edward W. Saunders, D, was challenged by his opponent in the election, the majority of the congressional investigating committee upheld the challenge.

They concluded that the Virginia law of 1908 was null and void because it did not conform with the federal law of January 16, 1901, or with the constitution of Virginia, and that the district should be regarded as including the counties that were a part of it before enactment of the 1908 state legislation. In that case Saunders's opponent would have had a majority of the votes, so the committee recommended that he be seated. For the first time, it appeared that the districting legislation would be enforced, but the House did not take action on the committee's report and Saunders's challenger was not seated.

Court Action on Redistricting

After the long and desultory battle over reapportionment in the 1920s, those who were unhappy over the inaction of Congress and the state legislatures began taking their cases to court. At first, the protestors had no luck. But as the population disparity grew in both federal and state legislative districts and the Supreme Court began to show a tendency to intervene, the objectors were more successful.

Finally, in a series of decisions beginning with *Baker v. Carr* in 1962 (369 U.S. 186) the Court exerted great influence over the redistricting process, ordering that congressional districts as well as state and local legislative districts be drawn so that their populations would be as nearly equal as possible.

Supreme Court's 1932 Decision

Baker v. Carr essentially reversed the direction the Court had taken in 1932. *Wood v. Broom* (287 U.S. 1) was a case challenging the constitutionality of a Mississippi redistricting law. The question was whether the 1911 federal redistricting act—which required that districts be separate, compact, contiguous, and equally populated and which had been neither specifically repealed nor reaffirmed in the 1929 reapportionment act—was still in effect.

Speaking for the Court, Chief Justice Charles Evans Hughes ruled that the 1911 act, in effect, had expired with the approval of the 1929 apportionment act and that the standards of the 1911 act therefore were no longer applicable. The Court reversed the decision of a lower federal court, which had permanently enjoined elections under the new Mississippi redistricting act because it violated the standards of the 1911 act.

That the Supreme Court upheld a state law that failed to provide for districts of equal population was almost less important than the minority opinion that the Court should not have heard the case. Justices Louis D. Brandeis, Harlan F. Stone, Owen J. Roberts, and Benjamin N. Cardozo, while concurring in the majority opinion, said they would have dismissed the Wood suit for "want of equity." The "want-of-equity" phrase in this context suggested a policy of judicial self-limitation with respect to the entire question of judicial involvement in essentially "political" questions.

"Political Thicket"

Not until 1946, in *Colegrove v. Green* (328 U.S. 549), did the Court again rule in a significant case dealing with congressional redistricting. The case was brought by Kenneth Colegrove, a political science professor at Northwestern University, who alleged that congressional districts in Illinois, which varied between 112,116 and 914,053 in population, were so unequal that they violated the Fourteenth Amendment's guarantee of equal protection of the laws. A seven-man Supreme Court divided 4-3 in dismissing the suit.

Justice Felix Frankfurter gave the opinion of the Court, speaking for himself and Justices Stanley F. Reed and Harold H. Burton. Frankfurter's opinion cited *Wood v. Broom* to indicate that Congress had deliberately removed the standard set by the 1911 act. "We also agree," he said, "with the four Justices [Brandeis, Stone, Roberts, and Cardozo] who were of the opinion that the bill in *Wood v. Broom* should be 'dismissed for want of equity.' " The issue, Frankfurter said, was

> of a peculiarly political nature and therefore not meant for judicial interpretation.... The short of it is that the Constitution has conferred upon Congress exclusive authority to secure fair representation by the states in the popular House and has left to that House determination whether states have fulfilled their responsibility. If Congress failed in exercising its powers, whereby standards of fairness are offended, the remedy lies ultimately with the people.... To sustain this action would cut very deep into the very being of Congress. Courts ought not to enter this political thicket. The remedy for unfairness in districting is to secure state legislatures that will apportion properly, or to invoke the ample powers of Congress.

Frankfurter also said that the Court could not affirmatively remap congressional districts and that elections at large would be politically undesirable.

In a dissenting opinion Justice Hugo L. Black, joined by Justices William O. Douglas and Frank Murphy, maintained that the district court did have jurisdiction over congressional redistricting. The three justices cited as evidence a section of the U.S. Code that allowed district courts to redress deprivations of constitutional rights occurring through action of the states. Black's opinion also rested on an earlier case in which the Court had indicated that federal constitutional questions, unless "frivolous," fall under the jurisdiction of the federal courts. Black asserted that the appellants had standing to sue and that the population disparities violated the equal protection clause of the Fourteenth Amendment.

With the Court split 3-3 on whether the judiciary had or should exercise jurisdiction, Justice Wiley B. Rutledge cast the deciding vote in *Colegrove v. Green*. On the question of justiciability, Rutledge agreed with Black, Douglas, and Murphy that the issue could be considered by the federal courts. Thus a majority of the Court participating in the *Colegrove* case felt that congressional redistricting cases were justiciable.

Yet on the question of granting relief in this specific instance, Rutledge agreed with Frankfurter, Reed, and Burton that the case should be dismissed. He pointed out that four of the nine justices in *Wood v. Broom* had felt that dismissal should be for want of equity. Rutledge saw a "want-of-equity" situation in *Colegrove v. Green* as well. "I think the gravity of the constitutional questions raised [are] so great, together with the possibility of collision [with the political departments of the government], that the admonition [against avoidable constitutional decision] is appropriate to be followed here," Rutledge said. Jurisdiction, he thought, should be exercised "only in the most compelling circumstances." He thought that "the shortness of time remaining [before the forthcoming election] makes it doubtful whether action could or would be taken in time to secure for petitioners the effective relief they seek." Rutledge warned that congressional elections at large would deprive citizens of representation by districts, "which the prevailing policy of Congress demands." In the case of at-large elections, he said, "the cure sought may be worse than the disease." For all these reasons he concluded that the case was "one in which the Court may properly, and should, decline to exercise its jurisdiction."

Changing Views

In the ensuing years, law professors, political scientists, and other commentators expressed growing criticism of the *Colegrove* doctrine and growing impatience with the Supreme Court's reluctance to intervene in redistricting disputes. At the same time, the membership of the Court was changing, and the new members were more inclined toward judicial action on redistricting.

In the 1950s the Court decided two cases that laid some groundwork for its subsequent reapportionment decisions. The first was *Brown v. Board of Education* (347 U.S. 483, 1954), the historic school desegregation case, in which the Court decided that an individual citizen could assert a right to equal protection of the laws under the Fourteenth Amendment, contrary to the "separate but equal" doctrine of public facilities for white and black citizens. Six years later, in *Gomillion v. Lightfoot* (364 U.S. 339, 1960), the Court held that the Alabama Legislature could not draw the city limits of Tuskegee so as to exclude nearly every black vote. In his opinion, Justice Frankfurter drew a clear line between redistricting challenges based on the Fourteenth Amendment, such as *Colegrove,* and Fifteenth Amendment challenges to discriminatory redistricting, as in *Gomillion.* But Justice Charles E. Whittaker said that the equal protection clause was the proper constitutional basis for the

decision. One commentator later remarked that *Gomillion* amounted to a "dragon" in the "political thicket" of *Colegrove.*

By 1962 only three members of the *Colegrove* Court remained: Justices Black and Douglas, dissenters in that case, and Justice Frankfurter, aging spokesman for restraint in the exercise of judicial power.

By then it was clear that malapportionment within the states no longer could be ignored. By 1960 not a single state legislative body existed in which there was not at least a 2-to-1 population disparity between the most and the least heavily populated districts. For example, the disparity was 242-1 in the Connecticut House, 223-1 in the Nevada Senate, 141-1 in the Rhode Island Senate, and 9-1 in the Georgia Senate. Studies of the effective vote of large and small counties in state legislatures between 1910 and 1960 showed that the effective vote of the most populous counties had slipped while their percentage of the national population had more than doubled. The most lightly populated counties, on the other hand, advanced from a position of slight overrepresentation to one of extreme overrepresentation, holding almost twice as many seats as they would be entitled to by population size alone. Predictably, the rural-dominated state legislatures resisted every move toward reapportioning state legislative districts to reflect new population patterns.

Population imbalance among congressional districts was substantially lopsided but by no means so gross. In Texas the 1960 census showed the most heavily populated district had four times as many inhabitants as the most lightly populated. Arizona, Maryland, and Ohio each had at least one district with three times as many inhabitants as the least populated. In most cases, rural areas benefited from the population imbalance in congressional districts. As a result of the postwar population movement out of central cities to the surrounding areas, the suburbs were the most under-represented.

Baker v. Carr

Against this background a group of Tennessee city dwellers successfully broke the longstanding precedent against federal court involvement in legislative apportionment problems. For more than half a century, since 1901, the Tennessee Legislature had refused to reapportion itself, even though a decennial reapportionment based on population was specifically required by the state's constitution. In the meantime, Tennessee's population had grown and shifted dramatically to urban areas. By 1960 the House legislative districts ranged from 3,454 to 36,031 in population, while the Senate districts ranged from 39,727 to 108,094. Appeals by urban residents to the rural-controlled Tennessee Legislature proved fruitless. A suit brought in the state courts to force reapportionment was rejected on grounds that the courts should stay out of legislative matters.

City dwellers then appealed to the federal courts, stating that they had no redress: the Legislature had refused to act for more than half a century, the state courts had refused to intervene, and Tennessee had no referendum or initiative laws. They charged that there was "a debasement of their votes by virtue of the incorrect, obsolete and unconstitutional apportionment" to such an extent that they were being deprived of their right to "equal protection of the laws" under the Fourteenth Amendment. (The Fourteenth Amendment reads, in part: "No state shall . . . deny to any person within its jurisdiction the equal protection of the laws.")

The Supreme Court on March 26, 1962, handed down its historic decision in *Baker v. Carr,* ruling in favor of the Tennessee city dwellers by a 6-2 margin. In the majority opinion, Justice William J. Brennan, Jr., emphasized that the federal judiciary had the power to review the apportionment of state legislatures under the Fourteenth Amendment's equal protection clause. "The mere fact that a suit seeks protection as a political right," Brennan wrote, "does not mean that it presents a political question" that the courts should avoid.

In a vigorous dissent, Justice Frankfurter said the majority decision constituted "a massive repudiation of the experience of our whole past" and was an assertion of "destructively novel judicial power." He contended that the lack of any clear basis for relief "catapults the lower courts" into a "mathematical quagmire." Frankfurter insisted that "there is not under our Constitution a judicial remedy for every political mischief." Appeal for relief, Frankfurter maintained, should not be made in the courts, but "to an informed civically militant electorate."

The Court had abandoned the view that malapportionment questions were outside its competence. But it stopped there and in *Baker v. Carr* did not address the merits of the challenge to the legislative districts.

Gray v. Sanders

The one-person, one-vote rule was set out first by the Court almost exactly one year after its decision in *Baker v. Carr.* But the case in which the announcement came did not involve congressional districts.

In the ruling in *Gray v. Sanders* (372 U.S. 368, 1963) the Court found that Georgia's county-unit primary system for electing state officials—a system that weighted votes to give advantage to rural districts in statewide primary elections—denied voters equal protection of the laws.

All votes in a statewide election must have equal weight, held the Court:

How then can one person be given twice or 10 times the voting power of another person in a statewide election merely because he lives in a rural area or because he lives in the smallest rural county? Once the geographical unit for which a representative is to be chosen is designated, all who participate in the election are to have an equal vote—whatever their race, whatever their sex, whatever their occupation, whatever their income, and wherever their home may be in that geographical unit. This is required by the Equal Protection Clause of the Fourteenth Amendment. The concept of "we the people" under the Constitution visualizes no preferred class of voters but equality among those who meet the basic qualification. The idea that every voter is equal to every other voter in his State, when he casts his ballot in favor of one of several competing candidates, underlies many of our decisions.... The conception of political equality from the Declaration of Independence to Lincoln's Gettysburg Address, to the Fifteenth, Seventeenth, and Nineteenth Amendments can mean only one thing—one person, one vote.

The Rule Applied

The Court's rulings in *Baker* and *Gray* concerned the equal weighting and counting of votes cast in state elections. In 1964, deciding the case of *Wesberry v. Sanders,* the Court applied the one-person, one-vote principle to congressional districts and set equality as the standard for congressional redistricting.

Shortly after the *Baker* decision was handed down, James P. Wesberry, Jr., an Atlanta resident and a member of the Georgia Senate, filed suit in federal court in Atlanta claiming that gross disparity in the population of Georgia's congressional districts violated Fourteenth Amendment rights of equal protection of the laws. At the time, Georgia districts ranged in population from 272,154 in the rural 9th District in the northeastern part of the state to 823,860 in the 5th District in Atlanta and its suburbs.

District lines had not been changed since 1931. The state's number of House seats remained the same in the interim, but Atlanta's district population—already high in 1931 compared with the others—had more than doubled in thirty years, making a 5th District vote worth about one-third that of a vote in the 9th.

On June 20, 1962, the three-judge federal court divided 2-1 in dismissing Wesberry's suit. The majority reasoned that the precedent of *Colegrove* still controlled in congressional district cases. The judges cautioned against federal judicial interference with Congress and against "depriving others of the right to vote" if the suit should result in at-large elections. They suggested that the Georgia Legislature (under court order to reapportion itself) or the U.S. Congress might better provide relief. Wesberry then appealed to the Supreme Court, which heard arguments in the case in November 1963.

On February 17, 1964, the Supreme Court ruled in *Wesberry v. Sanders* (376 U.S. 1) that congressional districts must be substantially equal in population. The Court, which upheld Wesberry's challenge by a 6-3 decision, based its ruling on the history and wording of Article I, Section 2, of the Constitution, which states that representatives shall be apportioned among the states according to their respective numbers and be chosen by the people of the several states. This language, the Court stated, meant that "as nearly as is practicable, one man's vote in a congressional election is to be worth as much as another's."

The majority opinion, written by Justice Black and supported by Chief Justice Earl Warren and Justices Brennan, Douglas, Arthur J. Goldberg, and Byron R. White, said: "While it may not be possible to draw congressional districts with mathematical precision, that is no excuse for ignoring our Constitution's plain objective of making equal representation for equal numbers of people the fundamental goal for the House of Representatives."

In a strongly worded dissent, Justice John M. Harlan asserted that the Constitution did not establish population as the only criterion of congressional districting and that the subject was left by the Constitution to the discretion of the states, subject only to the supervisory power of Congress. "The constitutional right which the Court creates is manufactured out of whole cloth," Harlan concluded.

The *Wesberry* opinion established no precise standards for districting beyond declaring that districts must be as nearly equal in population "as is practicable." In his dissent, Harlan suggested that a disparity of more than 100,000 between a state's largest and smallest districts would "presumably" violate the equality standard enunciated by the majority. On that basis, Harlan estimated, the districts of thirty-seven states with 398 representatives would be unconstitutional, "leaving a constitutional House of 37 members now sitting."

Neither did the Court's decision make any reference to gerrymandering, since it discussed only the population, not the shape of districts. In a separate districting opinion handed down the same day as *Wesberry,* the Court dismissed a challenge to congressional districts in New York City, which had been brought by voters who charged that Manhattan's "silk-stocking" 17th District had been gerrymandered to exclude blacks and Puerto Ricans.

Strict Equality

Five years elapsed between *Wesberry v. Sanders* and the Court's next application of constitutional standards to congressional districting. In 1967 the Court hinted at the strict stance it would adopt two years later. With two unsigned opinions, the Court sent back to Indiana and Missouri for revision those two states' congressional redistricting plans because they allowed variations of as much as 20 percent from the average district population.

Two years later Missouri's revised plan returned to the Court for full review. With its decision in *Kirkpatrick v. Preisler* (385 U.S. 450, 1969), the Court by a 6-3 vote rejected the plan. It was unacceptable, held the majority, because it allowed a variation of as much as 3.1 percent from perfectly equal population districts.

The Court thus made clear its stringent application of "one person, one vote" to congressional redistricting. Minor deviations from the strict equal-population principle were permissible only when the state provided substantial evidence that the variation was unavoidable.

Writing for the Court, Justice Brennan declared that there was no "fixed numerical or percentage population variance small enough to be considered *de minimis* and to satisfy without question the 'as nearly as practicable' standard." He wrote, "Equal representation for equal numbers of people is a principle designed to prevent debasement of voting power and diminution of access to elected Representatives. Toleration of even small deviations detracts from these purposes."

The only permissible variances in population, the Court ruled, were those that were unavoidable despite the effort to achieve absolute equality or those that could be legally justified. The variances in Missouri could have been avoided, the Court said.

None of Missouri's arguments for the plan qualified as "legally acceptable" justifications. The Court rejected the argument that population variance was necessary to allow representation of distinct interest groups. It said that acceptance of such variances to produce districts with specific interests was "antithetical" to the basic purpose of equal representation.

Justice White dissented from the majority opinion, which he characterized as "an unduly rigid and unwarranted application of the Equal Protection Clause which will unnecessarily involve the courts in the abrasive task of drawing district lines." White added that some "acceptably small" population variance could be established. He indicated that considerations of existing political boundaries and geographical compactness could justify to him some variation from "absolute equality" of population.

Justice Harlan, joined by Justice Potter Stewart, dissented, saying that "whatever room remained under this Court's prior decisions for the free play of the political process in matters of reapportionment is now all but eliminated by today's Draconian judgments."

Practical Results

As a result of the Court's decisions of the 1960s, nearly every state was forced to redraw its congressional district lines—sometimes more than once. By the end of the decade, thirty-nine of the forty-five states with more than one representative had made the necessary adjustments.

However, the effect of the one-person, one-vote standard on congressional districts did not bring about immediate equality in districts in the years 1964-1970. Most of the new districts were far from equal in population, because the only official population figures came from the 1960 census. Massive population shifts during the decade rendered most post-*Wesberry* efforts to achieve equality useless.

But following redistricting in 1971-1972, based on the 1970 census, the result achieved was that House members elected in November 1972 to the 93d Congress represented districts that differed only slightly in population from the state average. In 385 of the 435 districts, the district's variance was less than 1 percent from the state average district population.

By contrast, only 9 of the districts in the 88th Congress (elected in 1962) deviated less than 1 percent from the state average; 81 were between 1 and 5 percent; 87 from 5 to 10 percent; and in 236 districts the deviation was 10 percent or greater. Twenty-two House members were elected at large.

The Supreme Court made only one major ruling concerning congressional districts during the 1970s. On June 18, 1973, the Court declared the Texas congressional districts, as redrawn in 1971, unconstitutional because of excessive population variance among districts. The variance between the largest and smallest districts was 4.9872 percent. The Court returned the case to a three-judge federal panel, which adopted a new congressional district plan, effective October 17, 1973.

Precise Equality

Almost exactly ten years later, on June 22, 1983, the Supreme Court handed down another redistricting decision with sweeping implications. In a 5-4 decision, the Court ruled in *Karcher v. Daggett* (462 U.S. 725) that states must adhere as closely as possible to the one-person, one-vote standard and bear the burden of proving that deviations from precise population equality were made in pursuit of a legitimate goal. The decision overturned New Jersey's congressional map because the variation between the most populated and the least populated districts was 0.69 percent.

Brennan, who wrote the Court's opinion in *Baker* and *Kirkpatrick,* also wrote the opinion in *Karcher,* contending that population differences between districts "could have been avoided or significantly reduced with a good-faith effort to achieve population equality."

"Adopting any standard other than population equality, using the best census data available, would subtly erode the Constitution's ideal of equal representation," Brennan wrote.

> If state legislators knew that a certain *de minimis* level of population differences were acceptable, they would doubtless strive to achieve that level rather than equality. Furthermore, choosing a different standard would import a high degree of arbitrariness into the process of reviewing reapportionment plans. In this case, appellants argue that a maximum deviation of approximately 0.7 percent should be considered *de minimis*. If we accept that argument, how are we to regard deviations of 0.8 percent, 0.95 percent, 1.0 percent or 1.1 percent? . . . To accept the legitimacy of unjustified, though small population deviations in this case would mean to reject the basic premise of *Kirkpatrick* and *Wesberry*.

Brennan said that "any number of consistently applied legislative policies might justify" some population variation. These included "making districts compact, respecting municipal boundaries, preserving the cores of prior districts, and avoiding contests between incumbent Representatives." However, he cautioned, the state must show "with some specificity that a particular objective required the specific deviations in its plan, rather than simply relying on general assertions."

In his dissent Justice White criticized the majority for its "unreasonable insistence on an unattainable perfection in the equalizing of congressional districts." He warned that the decision would invite "further litigation of virtually every congressional redistricting plan in the nation"

The Court did not address the underlying political issue in the New Jersey case, which was that its map had been drawn to serve Democratic interests. As a partisan gerrymander, the map had few peers, boasting some of the most oddly shaped districts in the country. One constituency, known as the "fishhook" by its detractors, twisted through central New Jersey's industrial landscape, picking up Democratic voters along the way. Another stretched from the suburbs of New York to the fringes of Trenton.

In separate dissents Justices Lewis F. Powell, Jr., and John Paul Stevens broadly hinted that they were willing to hear constitutional challenges to instances of partisan gerrymandering. "A legislator cannot represent his constituents properly—nor can voters from a fragmented district exercise the ballot intelligently—when a voting district is nothing more than an artificial unit divorced from, and indeed often in conflict with, the various communities established in the State," wrote Powell.

The Court's opportunity to address that question came in *Davis v. Bandemer* (478 U.S. 109). On June 30, 1986, the Court ruled that political gerrymanders are subject to constitutional review by federal courts, even if the disputed districts meet the "one person, one vote" test. The case arose from a challenge by Indiana Democrats who argued that the Republican-drawn map so heavily favored the Republican party that Democrats were denied appropriate representation. But the Court rejected the Democrats' challenge to the alleged gerrymander, saying that one election was insufficient to prove unconstitutional discrimination.

Congress and Redistricting

Congress made several attempts in the post-World War II period to enact new legislation on redistricting. Only one of these efforts was successful—enactment of a measure barring at-large elections in states with more than one representative.

On January 9, 1951, President Harry S Truman, upon presentation of the official state population figures of the 1950 census, asked for changes in existing law to tighten federal control of state redistricting. Specifically, he asked for a ban on gerrymandering, an end to at-large seats in states having more than one representative, and a sharp reduction in the huge differences in size among congressional districts within most states.

On behalf of the administration, Emanuel Celler, D-N.Y., chairman of the House Judiciary Committee, introduced a bill to require compact and contiguous congressional districts that would not vary by more than 15 percent between districts within a state. The bill also eliminated at-large seats and made redistricting mandatory every ten years in accordance with population changes. But the House Judiciary Committee took no action on the proposals.

Representative Celler regularly introduced his bill throughout the 1950s and early 1960s, but it made no headway until the Supreme Court handed down the *Wesberry* decision in 1964. On June 24, 1964, a Celler bill was approved by a House Judiciary subcommittee. But the full committee did not act on the bill before adjournment of Congress.

On March 16, 1965, the House finally passed a redistricting bill. It established 15 percent as the maximum percentage by which a congressional district's population might deviate from the average size of the state's districts, prohibited at-large elections for any state with more than one House seat, required that districts be composed of "contiguous territory in as compact form as practicable," and forbade more than one redistricting of a state between decennial censuses. A major reason for House approval of Celler's bill appeared to be a desire to gain protection from Court imposition of even more rigid criteria. But the measure encountered difficulties in the Senate Judiciary Committee. After considerable wrangling over its provisions, the committee voted to report the bill without

precise agreement on its wording. No report was ever filed by the committee.

In 1967 a redistricting bill was passed by both the Senate and the House, but not in the same form. And the bill had a purpose different from that of previous bills dealing with the subject. Instead of trying to establish standards of fairness in drawing district lines, the chief purpose in 1967 was to prevent the courts from ordering redistricting of House seats or from ordering any state to hold elections at large—a procedure that many incumbent representatives feared—until after the House had been reapportioned on the basis of the 1970 census.

A combination of liberal Democrats and Republicans in the Senate managed to defeat the conference report November 8, by a vote of 22-55. Liberals favored court action, which they believed would eliminate many conservative rural districts, while Republicans felt that redistricted areas, especially in the growing suburbs, would elect more Republicans than Democrats.

To avoid at-large elections, the Senate added a rider to a House-passed private bill. Under the rider, at-large elections of U.S. representatives were banned in all states entitled to more than one representative, with the exceptions of New Mexico and Hawaii. Those states had a tradition of electing their two representatives at large. Both of them, however, soon passed districting laws—New Mexico for the 1968 elections and Hawaii for 1970.

In 1971 Celler introduced a new version of his proposed redistricting legislation. Although the House Judiciary Committee reported the measure favorably, no further action was taken on the bill, and it died at the end of the 92d Congress.

After the 1960 census, an attempt had been made to increase the size of the House to avoid some of the losses of seats that several states would otherwise suffer. By a vote of 12-14, the House Judiciary Committee on September 9, 1961, rejected a motion to recommend enlarging the House to 453 seats. And by a vote of 14-15, the same committee rejected a bill reported by a subcommittee that would have increased the permanent size of the House to 438.

Voting Rights Act

One form of gerrymandering is expressly forbidden by law: redistricting for the purpose of racial discrimination. The Voting Rights Act of 1965, extended in 1970, 1975, and 1982, banned redistricting that diluted the voting strength of black communities. Other minorities, including Hispanics, Asian-Americans, American Indians, and native Alaskans subsequently were brought under the protection of the law.

The law originally was aimed at those southern states where blacks had long been targets of discrimination. At the time the original law was passed, racial redistricting was not a great problem because black voting strength was minimal. However, with the enhancement of registration and voting rights for blacks, lawmakers feared that affected states would, through gerrymandering, divide black communities among several congressional districts and reduce the chances of electing black representatives. That concern resulted in Section 5, the preclearance provisions of the act; at present sixteen states need all or part of their redistricting plans approved by the federal government under the terms of the 1965 Voting Rights Act.

The act called for any "state or political subdivision" to be subject to federal examination if the U.S. attorney general found that a test or device, such as a literacy test, was used as a prerequisite for voting in the November 1, 1964, election, and if less than 50 percent of the voting-age

population was registered in a jurisdiction or less than 50 percent of those registered voted for president.

At that time, tests for literacy and moral character were not uncommon. In Mississippi, an applicant for voter registration had to show an ability to "read and write any section of the constitution of this state and give a reasonable interpretation thereof to the county registrar. . . . He must also show good moral character."

When the law initially was passed, the states subject to federal scrutiny (as outlined in Section 5 of the act) were Alabama, Georgia, Louisiana, Mississippi, South Carolina, and Virginia, and portions of Arizona, North Carolina, and Hawaii. In subsequent years, additional areas were added to the so-called Section 5 list, including all of Alaska and Texas, the rest of Arizona and parts of California, Florida, Michigan, New Hampshire, New York, and South Dakota.

Any change in election-related laws in these areas must be approved—or "precleared," in legal jargon—either by the Justice Department or by the federal district court in Washington, D.C.

In 1975 Congress amended the law to give further protection to non-English-speaking minorities. The amendment extended preclearance scrutiny to include several states with large Hispanic or Native American populations. Preclearance would be triggered (1) if the Census Bureau determined that more than 5 percent of a jurisdiction's voting-age population was of a single language minority; (2) if election materials had been printed only in English for the 1972 presidential election; and (3) if less than 50 percent of the voting-age population had registered for or voted in the 1972 presidential election.

In 1982 the law was extended for twenty-five years. At the same time, states were exempted from preclearance if they could show that no "test or device" laws had been attempted in the last ten years and that positive steps had been taken to improve voting rights for minorities. A number of states that at one time or another since 1964 have been covered under Section 5 have won exemption from preclearance: Hawaii, Colorado, Connecticut, Idaho, Massachusetts, Wyoming, Maine, New Mexico, and Oklahoma.

States subject to preclearance typically send their redistricting plans to the Justice Department, saving the litigation costs involved in taking a matter directly to the federal district court. The Justice Department has sixty days to approve or disallow the plan. Justice officials may request additional materials from a state; once the information is received, the department has an additional sixty days to assess the plan. If it fails to meet that deadline, the plan stands as approved by the state.

In assessing a redistricting plan, the Justice Department searches for evidence of discrimination against a minority group that has a reasonable chance of electing a candidate of its choice. For example, federal officials would look suspiciously on a remap that split a concentrated 65 percent minority population into two districts.

While Section 2 of the Voting Rights Act stipulates that a law must be changed if it is discriminatory, the Justice Department, in assessing a remap, traditionally has looked more at the comparative change between the old and the new maps to determine if minority voters would be worse off under a new plan than they are under the current plan. During the 1980s, however, the Justice Department adopted new regulations that have been interpreted by some as expanding the definition of racially discriminatory redistricting. Where previously a new map passed muster as long as it did not diminish a minority's preexisting voting strength, the new Justice regulations, if upheld by the courts, may *require* a state

with racial-bloc voting to draw a district in which minorities are a majority, if such a district can be created.

If the department strikes down a remap, a state may take its case to federal court. Should Justice officials uphold a plan that a minority group believes is discriminatory, that grievance may be pursued in court.

If history repeats itself, the Justice Department, courts, and state legislatures in the South had better prepare for a lot of overtime during the coming redistricting season. In the 1980s remap round, every southern state covered under Section 5 had at least one plan struck down, either by the Justice Department or in federal court.

Procedures for Remaps

Although congressional redistricting is an extraordinary, once-a-decade activity, there is nothing particularly unusual about the legislative process that produces the maps in the majority of states.

In the typical state, redistricting work generally follows the textbook "how a bill becomes law" formula: new congressional district parameters are proposed in the form of legislation, which is reviewed by committees in both houses of the state legislature. Some states set up special redistricting committees, while others channel the bills through existing panels—with titles such as Election Law, State Government, or Justice—that normally deal with election-related issues. The bills are then debated on the floors of the houses, where they are subject to amendment. The legislature's final product is sent to the governor, whose veto may be overridden by a two-thirds majority in the legislature. The entire process in these states must be completed in time for the 1992 congressional elections.

This textbook formula governs redistricting in thirty states: Alabama, Arizona, Arkansas, California, Colorado, Florida, Georgia, Kansas, Louisiana, Maryland, Massachusetts, Michigan, Minnesota, Mississippi, Missouri, Nebraska, Nevada, New Hampshire, New Jersey, New Mexico, Ohio, Oklahoma, Oregon, Pennsylvania, Rhode Island, South Carolina, Texas, Utah, Virginia, and Wisconsin.

At Arm's Length

Five states turn the principal responsibility for redistricting over to an independent or quasi-independent commission or state agency. Two states, Hawaii and Montana, have laws that completely exclude the state legislative process from redistricting.

Hawaii. In early 1991 a nine-member reapportionment committee will be appointed in Hawaii. The majority and minority leaders of both houses of the Legislature will appoint two members each; the ninth member will then be chosen by the committee members. The committee will have 150 days to redraw the congressional map. Its plan will then be presented to the lieutenant governor for publication into law.

Montana. A five-member commission will be empaneled to craft a plan within ninety days of the 1991 release of census data. The majority and minority leaders of the Legislature will appoint one member each; the empaneled members then choose the fifth member. The final plan is sent to the Montana secretary of state and becomes law. However, Montana may lose one of its two House seats after the 1990 census, rendering this redistricting procedure moot.

Three other "commission" states, Connecticut, Iowa, and Washington, provide their legislators some limited say over the outcome of redistricting.

Connecticut. An eight-member legislative reapportionment committee is selected, in equal numbers, by the Democratic and Republican leaders of both houses of the state Legislature; the committee has until August 1, 1991, to report a congressional plan to the Legislature. If it fails to do so, a nine-member reapportionment commission will be created. Again, eight members of this commission would be appointed, in equal numbers, by the major party leaders in the Legislature; the ninth member would then be selected by the other eight commissioners. The commission would have to submit a plan by October 31, 1991, at which time it would go directly into law.

Iowa. Responsibility for redrawing the lines is given to the state Legislature's nonpartisan Legislative Services Bureau, which must submit a plan by April 1, 1991. The Legislature is entitled to reject the first two plans presented by the bureau, then may amend the third proposed plan. However, if the Legislature should stalemate on a third plan, the state Supreme Court would take over the process.

Washington. The five-member Washington State Redistricting Commission will be empaneled by the end of January 1991. One member will be chosen by each of the leaders of the state Legislature's party caucuses (no current legislators may serve on the commission); these appointees will then pick a fifth member to serve as chairman. The commission will have until January 1, 1992, to present a congressional plan to the Legislature, which may make only minor alterations that must pass by a two-thirds vote in each house. If the commission fails to meet its deadline, the remap will be turned over to the state Supreme Court, which will have the final say.

Other states may join the "commission club" in time for the next round of redistricting. The most prominent example is California, where the June 1990 primary ballot includes a proposal to create a re-districting commission; the initiative is backed by a number of Republicans who worry about a repeat of the 1980s gerry-mander by the Democratic-controlled Leg-islature. In Utah, the Democratic minority is pushing a similar proposition.

The Quirks of the Process

Even some of those states that provide their legislatures with the major responsibil-ity for congressional redistricting have pro-visions and quirks that set them apart from the "textbook" formula states.

Idaho. The Legislature is not required to deal with redistricting until its 1993 session. Also, only a simple majority vote is needed to override a governor's veto of redistricting legislation.

Illinois. A three-fifths vote of the Leg-islature is needed to override a guberna-torial redistricting veto.

Indiana. If the Legislature fails to meet an April 30, 1991, deadline for redistricting, the remap will be done by a redistricting commission made up of a representative of the governor, the majority leaders of the state Senate and House, and the chairmen of both houses' reapportionment commit-tees. The commission's final plan will be-come law until the next session of the state Legislature.

Kentucky. The Legislature is not re-quired to complete congressional redistrict-ing until spring 1993.

Maine. The redistricting process is ini-tiated by a fifteen-member commission,

which presents a draft plan to the Legisla-ture. The members are appointed as follows: three members each by the Democratic and Republican leaders in the state House; two each by the party leaders in the state Senate; the chairmen (or designees) of the state Democratic and Republican parties; and three members of the public, one each selected by the state party chairmen, and a third selected by the other two citizen mem-bers. The commission's redistricting pro-posal is advisory only; the Legislature is not obliged to accept it without amendment.

New York. The state has a permanent legislative task force on reapportionment, which has two co-chairmen who are individ-ually appointed by the majority leaders of the state Senate (currently controlled by Republicans) and Assembly (which has a Democratic majority). This task force draws up the initial redistricting proposal, which then goes through the normal state legislative process.

North Carolina. The governor has no veto power over redistricting—or in any other matter. North Carolina is the only state whose governor has no legislative veto power.

Tennessee and West Virginia. A simple majority is needed to override any guberna-torial veto of a redistricting plan.

For the nation's six least populous states—Alaska, Delaware, North Dakota, South Dakota, Vermont, and Wyoming—congressional redistricting is not an issue. Each of these states has a single at-large House district. Population projections indi-cate that Montana may join their ranks after the 1990 census.

2

Political Parties and Redistricting

As the 1990's round of congressional redistricting approaches, a question is coming into focus: Can the Republican party find a way to convert demographic trends it sees as favorable into a larger presence—perhaps even a majority—in the House of Representatives?

The decennial process of line drawing is always fraught with controversy, and GOP officials have raised the stakes even higher than usual by talking of the redistricting after the 1990 census as their party's last chance this century to shake its minority status in the House. But Republicans will have to succeed in all aspects associated with redistricting: the 1990 elections, legislative maneuvering to prevent gerrymandering, understanding the implications of strategies that protect GOP incumbents as well as Democratic ones, and staying up to speed with the technology needed to draw the maps.

That will be a tall order. After all, Democrats are not going to be sitting around waiting to see what Republicans will do. They will form their own strategies to shape the redistricting process to preserve their comfortable House majority, which currently stands at eighty-two seats (258-176, with one vacancy). Redistricting is one of the most intensely political elements of American politics.

One of the earliest tests will come in November 1990. Both parties are spending millions of dollars to influence redistricting by winning state-level elections. In almost every state, congressional district lines are drawn by the state legislature, with the governor holding veto power.

Winners and Losers

Since the Democrats began their unbroken control of the House in 1955, thirty-seven House seats have moved from the Frost Belt to the Sun Belt. Various apportionment estimates show that probably fifteen to twenty more seats will be heading southward and westward for the 1990s. *(Map, p. 34)*

California, Texas, and Florida are almost certain to be big winners. Various projections show each of them gaining at least three House seats, with California adding six or seven. Meanwhile, the Frost Belt heavyweights—New York, Pennsylvania, Illinois, Ohio, and Michigan—are almost certain to be big losers. All are projected to lose at least two seats each.

These projections, however, are just educated guesses. The exact state-by-state apportionment of House seats will be determined after the 1990 census. "There is almost bound to be a difference between

1990 Reapportionment:
Projected Gainers and Losers

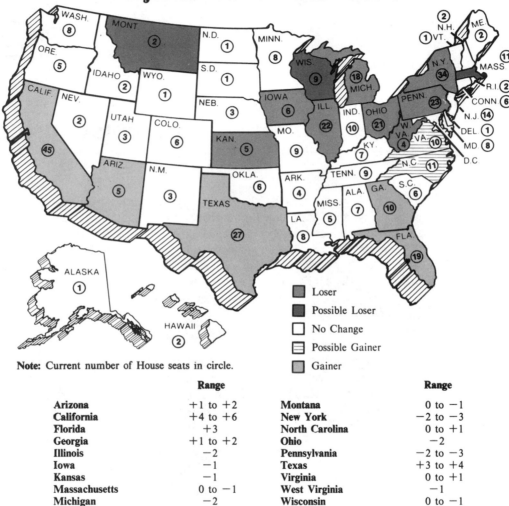

Note: Current number of House seats in circle.

Loser
Possible Loser
No Change
Possible Gainer
Gainer

	Range		Range
Arizona	+1 to +2	**Montana**	0 to −1
California	+4 to +6	**New York**	−2 to −3
Florida	+3	**North Carolina**	0 to +1
Georgia	+1 to +2	**Ohio**	−2
Illinois	−2	**Pennsylvania**	−2 to −3
Iowa	−1	**Texas**	+3 to +4
Kansas	−1	**Virginia**	0 to +1
Massachusetts	0 to −1	**West Virginia**	−1
Michigan	−2	**Wisconsin**	0 to −1

NOTE: Chart based on four different sets of 1990 population projections. Three sets were used by the Congressional Research Service as the basis for figuring apportionment totals in an August 1988 report. The other set was computed by Kim Brace's Election Data Services this year. According to Brace, Kentucky and New Jersey are each also close to losing a seat.

projections and actual apportionment numbers," warned David C. Huckabee, an analyst with the Library of Congress's Congressional Research Service. In 1979 the Census Bureau projection of the nationwide population for 1980 was more than 5 million under what the census actually counted. In addition to the uncertainty surrounding population projections, there is an ongoing squabble over how to conduct an accurate census. *(See box, p. 36)*

Growth and Decline

If some of the fine points of the head-counting remain fuzzy, a few broad demographic trends are clear. Mid-decade Census Bureau population estimates found that the fastest-growing House districts are all in the South and the West.

Meanwhile, the movement within states from urban centers to suburbs is continuing, particularly to outer suburbs, frequently called exurbs. Most urban districts, especially those in the Frost Belt, are losing population. Census Bureau estimates for the 1980-1986 period show that of the eleven districts that lost the highest percentage of people in that time, eight were urban districts in Frost Belt cities—and Democrats represent all of them. *(Box, p. 39)*

Although districts losing population are often urban and minority dominated, there are a number of others in decline that are predominantly rural and small town and overwhelmingly white. Most of these lie in a broad swath that extends from upstate New York through industrial western Pennsylvania and the small cities and towns of the midwestern Farm Belt to the edge of the Rockies. They are districts such as Pennsylvania's 22d, West Virginia's 1st, Indiana's 5th, Michigan's 8th, Ohio's 18th, Illinois's 17th, Minnesota's 8th, and Iowa's 3d—all of which are held by Democrats. Overall, Democratic House strength is greatest in the nation's slower-growth districts. Democrats represent 76 percent of those districts that had lost population at mid-decade, 60 percent that had a slow growth rate (below the national 1980-1986 rate of 6.4 percent), and 55 percent that had a moderate growth rate (from 6.4 percent to 20 percent). Democrats represent just 29 percent of the districts that had a fast growth rate (20 percent and above).

Can Democrats Stem the Tide?

Will the 1992 elections be the time when demographics finally overwhelm the Democratic House majority? Not necessar-

ily, according to Tom Hofeller, director of redistricting for the National Republican Congressional Committee (NRCC). "The gerrymander overcometh all. What demographics give, legislatures can take away in the dead of the night."

To reduce the Democratic advantage to dictate the lines, Republicans say they must alter the political landscape. Right now, the GOP suffers a decided disadvantage. The major players in each state's redistricting process—the governor, the state Senate, and the state House—constitute a tripod. In each of the ten most populous states, Republicans control no more than one leg of the tripod. They hold the governorship in California, Texas, Florida, Illinois, and North Carolina, and the state Senate in New York, Pennsylvania, Ohio, and Michigan.

In most of these states, all three legs of the tripod will be up for election in 1990. "If we lose the leg," Hofeller said, "we're out of the game." When the Republicans in California failed to hold any part of the tripod a decade ago, Democratic control of the governorship and the state Legislature enabled the party to enact an unabashedly partisan map drawn by Democratic representative Phillip Burton (1964-1983). The artfully drawn lines offset population growth in GOP suburban areas to stretch a 22-21 Democratic edge within the delegation to a lopsided 28-17 Democratic advantage after the 1982 elections.

Although Democrats did not hold the governorship in California, in most of the country they approached the 1990 elections sitting in the catbird seat. Of the forty-four states with more than one House district, Democrats controlled the governorship and both chambers of the state legislature in fourteen states with 97 House districts; they control two of the three legs of the tripod in twenty other states with 280 House districts.

Simple Question, Tough Answer...

Counting the number of people in the United States has never been as easy as one, two, three, and that is not just because of logistical problems. When it comes to the decennial census, the political stakes are high, and so is the interest in how the count is conducted. The constitutionally mandated census does far more than supply demographic figures for curious statisticians. It provides crucial information that shapes the reapportionment of U.S. House seats among the states, the drawing of district boundaries for federal, state, and local public officials, and the distribution of certain federal funds.

"It goes straight to the heart of what we are about," said Rep. Tom Ridge, R-Pa., "and that is who votes, how we distribute power ... who should be included in the political community. That's why the Constitution mandated the census; not for demographic information, but to redistribute power, voting power."

This view has led Ridge and numerous others into a debate over the Census Bureau's approach to the 1990 count, because the bureau's stated goal has little to do with defining the "political community." Its mission, simply put, is to count everyone. "For every census we have counted everyone who is a resident. That is our determining factor," said James E. Gorman, bureau public information chief.

Some complain that the bureau's effort to count all people living in the United States has unfair political ramifications. In particular, members of Congress and other public officials have taken a strong interest in the traditional inclusion of illegal aliens in the census, and in a historical undercounting of certain groups, especially blacks.

Policy on Illegal Aliens

The inclusion of illegal aliens in the population figures used in reapportionment usually stirs heated debate in Congress. The Fourteenth Amendment states, "Representatives shall be apportioned among the several states according to their respective numbers, counting the whole number of persons in each state, excluding Indians not taxed." The Census Bureau has never attempted to exclude illegal aliens from the census—a policy very troubling to states that fear losing political clout to states with large numbers of illegal aliens. "At the national, state, and local level, the inclusion of illegal aliens ... in the population base for reapportionment ... dilutes the votes of citizens," Ridge said. His state may lose an additional House seat.

According to Rep. Thomas C. Sawyer, D-Ohio, the latest court ruling on the policy of counting all residents, "is only the most recent in a 200-year trail of precedent." This question has been visited "in many different forms, on many different occasions," he added, and "the conclusion at every turn seems to have been that it was the intent to count everybody."

The Census Bureau does not have a method for excluding illegal aliens, although it has studied some alternatives. Some supporters of the current policy say that any questions used to separate out illegal aliens could discourage others from responding, thus undermining the census' accuracy.

... Whom Should the Census Count?

Missing Persons

The expected undercount of minority groups is another problem that also receives considerable attention, although a recent legal settlement may ease pressure for a legislative solution. The Census Bureau estimated that it did not count 1.4 percent of the total population in 1980; the undercount was most significant in minority communities. For example, the bureau estimated that it missed roughly 5.9 percent of the nation's blacks. Many of the "missing" live in inner-city areas, so the undercount issue is a particular concern for major cities and for the Democrats who tend to represent them.

Making an accurate population count in a crowded and perhaps crime-ridden inner-city neighborhood can be difficult. Government census takers as well as those they are trying to count may view one another with suspicion or fear. In response, some urban politicians have urged the Census Bureau to use a statistical method to adjust the census figures for the undercount. The Commerce Department, of which the Census Bureau is a part, announced in 1987 that it would not make such an adjustment.

But a lawsuit filed by New York City, other state and local governments, and civil rights groups altered the outlook for an adjustment. On July 17, 1989, the Commerce and Justice departments announced a settlement in which Commerce would prepare for a possible adjustment, which would involve a "post-enumeration survey" conducted after the actual count. The survey could then be used to adjust the figures, if the Commerce secretary deems that appropriate.

A 1988 study by the Population Reference Bureau, a nonprofit research organization, concluded that an adjustment for the expected minority undercount would have little or no impact on reapportionment. "It is unlikely that an undercount for minorities would swing more than a couple of seats at best," said William P. O'Hare, director of policy studies for the organization. But O'Hare noted that the intrastate impact could be significant, giving urban areas in a state a boost against faster-growing suburbs in redistricting. This could occur in Michigan, for example, where two black-majority districts in Detroit have had significant population losses. An adjustment might not spare the state its expected loss of two House seats, but an adjusted count in Detroit might bolster efforts to maintain those two black districts.

Counting Overseas Personnel

The Commerce Department reversed a long-standing policy and will count in the 1990 census military personnel and dependents stationed overseas. "Historically we have not included them because the census is based on the concept of usual residence," said Charles Jones, associate director of the Census Bureau. "People overseas have a 'usual residence' overseas." An exception was made once in 1970 during the Vietnam War.

The Defense Department planned to conduct the count, which involved 1.2 million to 1.6 million people. For the purposes of reapportionment, overseas personnel most likely will be assigned to the state each individual considers home.

There is some thought that the current public focus on ethics in government might reduce the prospect of blatant gerrymandering. But GOP consultant Eddie Mahe is among the many who are skeptical of this view. "We're talking about power," he said. The participants in redistricting "will not be greatly disposed to be ladies and gentlemen. It will be no holds barred."

Partisan Maps, Sweetheart Maps

Basically there are two types of gerrymanders. One is the partisan gerrymander, where a single party draws the lines to its advantage. The other is the pro-incumbent (sometimes called the "bipartisan" or "sweetheart") gerrymander, where the lines are drawn to protect incumbents, with any gains or losses in the number of seats shared between the two parties. In states where control of the state government is divided, pro-incumbent gerrymanders are common.

In the eyes of some Republicans, either species of gerrymander ensures their continued minority status in the House. "If we allow ourselves to be ruthlessly gerrymandered in reapportionment as we did the last time," Republican National Committee (RNC) chairman Lee Atwater has said, "we can forget any legitimate reasonable chance of getting control of the U.S. House of Representatives until well into the next millenium."

Democrats contend that the GOP suffers from bad candidates, not bad district lines. Indeed, some academics maintain that the extent of gerrymandering and its impact on the composition of the House are exaggerated. Everett C. Ladd, the director of the Roper Center for Public Opinion at the University of Connecticut, said, "To a large extent, the population is voting without regard to party. So the precise location of the congressional district lines is not so important as it was in an earlier era."

"There are only a few states with all the conditions ripe for partisanship," added Bruce Cain, a political scientist at the University of California at Berkeley. Basically, the state must be fairly large and competitive politically, but with one party in complete control of the state government.

And for every case of partisan gerrymandering that worked, such as in California, there is another case where it backfired, such as in Indiana. Hoosier Republicans drew their remap in 1981 with the hope that it would turn the Democrats' congressional majority into a 7-3 GOP edge. Instead, what prevailed early in 1990 was 7-3 Democratic advantage.

In this era of extremely high incumbent reelection rates, redistricting does increase the possibility of turnover, because new district lines are drawn practically everywhere. It is a time when some House members choose to retire rather than face redesigned constituencies. But a pro-incumbent spin in much of the line drawing dampens the prospects for dramatic partisan turnover. "There'll be some Republican gerrymandering, some Democratic gerrymandering, and a lot of sweetheart gerrymandering," according to Bernard Grofman, a political scientist at the University of California at Irvine.

Sweetheart gerrymandering rarely attracts much attention. With satisfied incumbents of both parties portraying it as "good government," the media have no controversy to highlight. But this method of mapping has a powerful effect on the makeup of the House. "Districts get more Democratic for Democrats and more Republican for Republicans," said Hofeller. "Competition is minimized." Because the majority of House seats are controlled by Democrats, pro-incumbent line drawing helps perpetuate the Democratic House majority.

Two Sides of the Coin

Mid-decade district-by-district population estimates by the Census Bureau show that the fastest growing congressional districts in the country are generally Republican-oriented constituencies in the Sun Belt, while those losing population at the highest rate are Democratic-oriented districts in Frost Belt urban centers.

There are exceptions in each category, however. One of the districts growing at a fast pace is the Austin-based Texas 10th, which is represented in the House by Democrat J. J. "Jake" Pickle and which voted in the 1988 presidential election for Democrat Michael S. Dukakis. Meanwhile, one of the biggest population losers through the first half of the 1980s was the Illinois 18th in the heart of the Farm Belt; it voted for Republican George Bush and is home base for House Minority Leader Robert H. Michel.

The chart is based on Census Bureau estimates of population change in each district from 1980 to 1986 and published by the bureau in January 1988. The bureau warns that district estimates from split-district population centers are less precise than estimates from other parts of the country. No new district-by-district figures are expected before the results of the 1990 census are released.

LEADING POPULATION GAINERS

District (Location)	Percent Change, 1980-1986	Incumbent	Presidential Winner, 1988
Texas 26 (Fort Worth Suburbs)	+41.7%	Dick Armey (R)	Bush (69%)
Florida 11 (East—Melbourne)	+33.3	Bill Nelson (D)	Bush (70%)
Texas 10 (Central—Austin)	+33.2	J. J. "Jake" Pickle (D)	Dukakis (54%)
California 37 (Riverside County)	+33.1	Al McCandless (R)	Bush (61%)
Alaska At-Large	+32.8	Don Young (R)	Bush (60%)
Arizona 1 (Eastern Phoenix; Tempe; Mesa)	+32.7	John J. Rhodes III (R)	Bush (65%)
Florida 6 (North Central—Gainesville)	+32.5	Cliff Stearns (R)	Bush (60%)
Florida 12 (South Central—West Palm Beach)	+32.3	Tom Lewis (R)	Bush (64%)
Florida 14 (Southeast—Part of Palm Beach)	+31.5	Harry A. Johnston (D)	Bush (53%)
Florida 13 (Southwest—Sarasota)	+31.4	Porter Goss (R)	Bush (68%)

LEADING POPULATION LOSERS

District (Location)	Percent Change, 1980-1986	Incumbent	Presidential Winner, 1988
Michigan 13 (Downtown Detroit)	−13.6%	George W. Crockett, Jr. (D)	Dukakis (85%)
Pennsylvania 14 (Pittsburgh)	− 8.1	William J. Coyne (D)	Dukakis (72%)
New York 33 (West—Buffalo)	− 7.6	Henry J. Nowak (D)	Dukakis (66%)
Michigan 1 (North Central Detroit)	− 6.3	John Conyers, Jr. (D)	Dukakis (90%)
New York 18 (South Bronx)	− 6.2	Robert Garcia (D)	Dukakis (86%)
Michigan 17 (Northwest Detroit)	− 5.9	Sander M. Levin (D)	Dukakis (53%)
Illinois 17 (West—Rock Island)	− 5.8	Lane Evans (D)	Dukakis (53%)
Indiana 1 (Gary; Hammond)	− 5.8	Peter J. Visclosky (D)	Dukakis (59%)
Illinois 18 (Central—Peoria)	− 5.4	Robert H. Michel (R)	Bush (55%)
Michigan 14 (Detroit Suburbs—Warren)	− 5.3	Dennis M. Hertel (D)	Bush (56%)
Ohio 21 (Cleveland—East)	− 5.3	Louis Stokes (D)	Dukakis (80%)

1990: Round One

As each party prepares for redistricting, it focuses on three basic areas—the political, the technological, and the legal.

The political means simply the 1990 elections. For both sides, a strong showing at the polls is a necessary starting point for whatever follows. "Technology is interesting," GOP consultant Mahe said, and litigation can keep a party from being victimized by a redistricting plan that is "outrageous." But "redistricting is decided November 6."

Republicans planned to focus much of their energy on state legislative races. Party resources were to be targeted to states that will gain or lose seats in reapportionment, to states where Republicans either need to hold a legislative chamber or could conceivably pick one up, or to states where the GOP is in a legislative minority but could establish a large enough bloc to uphold a veto by a GOP governor.

The RNC has organized recruitment days for prospective state legislative candidates, bringing them to Washington to meet with RNC and White House officials. Vice President Dan Quayle was enlisted as the administration's point man in fund raising and campaigning for the party's legislative candidates in 1990.

For Democrats, successful redistricting also starts with the state legislators. "If you don't have members of the legislature," said Democratic National Committee (DNC) political director Paul Tully, "all other relative dimensions to the effort—legal, technical—are a lot less meaningful."

But Democrats are also carefully guarding another flank—their governorships. The Democratic advantage in governorships, as high as 34-16 in the mid-1980s, stood at 29-21 early in 1990. The gubernatorial races, Tully said, are "something we care more about than the contested U.S. Senate races in 1990."

Once the 1990 elections are over, the focus turns to the technical dimension. The DNC has formed a national umbrella group called the Democratic Working Group on Redistricting. Its purpose is to get Democrats with interest or expertise in redistricting involved in helping to equip state party leaders with the resources and expertise needed to handle the line-drawing process.

Anyone Can Play

Technology is one of the greatest areas of change since the last round of redistricting a decade ago. When states were redrawing their lines in the early 1980s, "it was done more on the back of envelopes," according to Kimball Brace, a Washington-based redistricting consultant. At that time computations were often done on large mainframe computers that worked relatively slowly and were available to only a handful of political insiders.

At present, mapping can be done more quickly and cheaply. With the increasing use and sophistication of personal computers, "It's possible for almost anyone who has a computer to do redistricting," Hofeller said. The Census Bureau also planned to make more demographic information available to would-be players in the redistricting process. For the first time, the bureau planned to offer block-by-block racial and ethnic data, as well as a computerized map of the United States broken down to the block level; the map is called "TIGER," short for Topologically Integrated Geographic Encoding and Referencing system.

Because of the advances in technology and informational detail, more players can be expected at the remapping table and there will be more different plans from which to choose. It will not be just the political insiders drawing maps. Business, labor, minority, and "good government" groups can devise their own plans for legislative consideration. With a more open process, negotiations over competing remap plans may become more complicated and protracted. With new technology, RNC chief counsel Ben Ginsberg pointed out, more sophisticated gerrymanders can be drawn. "The Phil Burton map in California will look like child's play," he said.

The Legal Realm

The Burton map met the one firm legal criterion required by the Supreme Court: that the districts be of equal population. Republicans complained that it was an egregious gerrymander, with odd-shaped districts that neither were drawn compactly nor respected community boundaries. But Burton could brag that his map was loyal to the Court's edict: the average variance in population between districts was only sixty-seven people.

The Court had entered the arena of population equality in the 1964 *Wesberry v. Sanders* decision, which ruled that congressional districts had to be "substantially equal" in population. Since then, a series of rulings significantly tightened the standard, so that now virtually no variance in population is allowed among districts within a state. Critics argue that the Court's obsession with the exactness of the numbers actually encourages gerrymandering, since it is often difficult to devise equal-sized districts without dividing communities or drawing the lines into tortured shapes. "It was good as originally intended," Bernard Grofman said, "but it's been carried to absurdity."

A second major area of litigation in the redistricting process involves minority representation. Blacks and Hispanics represent many districts that are losing population, but they are probably in a stronger legal position than they have ever been to protect their districts, and perhaps to carve out new ones. The 1982 amendments to the Voting Rights Act changed the criteria for proving racial gerrymandering. No longer does a plaintiff have to establish that there was an "intent" to dilute the clout of a particular voting bloc; the plaintiff merely has to show that was the "effect" of the remap.

With the greater threat of a lawsuit, legislatures are unlikely to eliminate a minority district. Their reluctance could create some touchy problems during the redistricting process, particularly for urban Democrats. If they are forced to eliminate a district represented by a black or Hispanic, or one represented by a white, the one held by the white is likely to go.

For Republicans, the big legal question these days is where the Supreme Court stands on the issue of partisan gerrymandering. The Court has not been shy about overturning redistricting plans that discriminate against racial minorities. But it is relatively new to the question of partisan gerrymandering—cases where the aggrieved is a political party rather than an individual.

The Court entered the picture in 1986, when it declared in *Davis v. Bandemer* (478 U.S. 109), a case involving a Republican legislative redistricting plan in Indiana, that partisan gerrymanders could be unconstitutional. However, the Court upheld the Indiana remap, and failed to outline clear standards that the political parties could use in challenging a plan on the grounds that it is a partisan gerrymander.

Republicans had hoped to get a better definition of such standards when they filed suit against the map drawn by the California Democrats. But in deciding *Eu v. San Francisco County Democratic Central Committee* (489 U.S. ——) in January 1989, the Court ruled without comment that the map did not constitute an unconstitutional partisan gerrymander. Even a favorable ruling for the GOP in *Eu* would have had little practical effect, since the lines were to be redrawn in two or three years anyway. But the decision clearly disappointed many Republicans, who had hoped to enlist the Court as an ally in the upcoming redistricting battle. Many Republicans felt that the California case was about as clear an example of partisan gerrymandering as they would get.

Republican Strategy

The administration of President George Bush has sought to spell out criteria for line drawing in an antigerrymandering initiative that was included in the president's campaign-reform package unveiled in late June 1989. The initiative, entitled "Fairness in Redistricting," appeared in a section of the package called "Reforming Unfair Advantages." The initiative calls for line drawing that would "adhere to compactness standards and follow established community boundaries," and for fully enforcing the Voting Rights Act, as amended in 1982.

Republicans are promoting their proposal as one that would increase competition, but Democrats see it as a public relations stunt. "I don't know what it is," said California representative Vic Fazio, chairman of IMPAC 2000, a fund-raising group for Democratic legislative and gubernatorial candidates. "It's just a statement saying some nice things about redistricting. It's kind of window dressing."

"It's an attempt to expand the national Republican anti-Congress message into a related field," the DNC's Tully added. "It's one of the great attempts to take politics out of one of the most political processes imaginable."

Democrats are particularly upset with Bush's promise to protect minority districts. They see it as a cynical pitch for black and Hispanic votes that does not require the investment of much political capital. "Obvi-ously what the Republicans would like to do in some areas," Fazio said, "is put every black voter in one district, which would enhance their chances of winning the remaining districts. I think blacks would be mistaken to see it as an act of altruism."

The GOP's Hofeller counters that Republicans and minorities "are traveling down the same path because we're being disadvantaged by the same process. We're both sitting on the outside and trying to get a fair share of the pie."

Republicans may gain some advantage in redistricting through the decisions of federal district judges. If the legislature and the governor cannot agree on the lines in a particular state, the lines would likely have to be drawn by a federal court. In the last round of redistricting, however, federal panels tended to side with Democrats. Three-judge panels in Kansas, Michigan, Minnesota, and Missouri all produced 2-1 majorities for Democratic plans. So did the panel in Illinois, even though a majority of its members were GOP appointees.

The specter of a friendly federal court was a handy bargaining chip for Democratic legislators in many states in the early 1980s. But a decade of Republican appointments to the federal bench may have negated the Democrats' advantage. There have been numerous conservative appointments to federal judgeships in recent years. "We'll see it show up around redistricting and reapportionment," Tully said.

But Republicans were not publicly predicting that the courts will be their safety net. They should provide the party with "more cover than 1981 and 1982," Mahe said, but "anytime you try to win in court, that's a marginal strategy."

While the parties focus on the 1990 elections and the orgy of line drawing to follow, it should be remembered that the political backdrop of the 1992 elections will likely have as much impact on the outcome of House contests as will the new lines. In the postreapportionment elections of 1982, Republican hopes of picking up ground in the House were blunted by the recession. The political environment in 1992 could be more favorable. But since World War II, Republicans have never gained more than fourteen seats in a year that a GOP president was running for reelection.

Unless the GOP enjoys much more success in 1990 House elections than is now foreseen, a 1992 gain in the fourteen-seat range would bring the party up short in its long quest for a House majority.

3

Incumbency and Redistricting

In redistricting, the decennial exercise of political musical chairs, no member of the House of Representatives ever wants to be left without a seat. The remapping will not begin in earnest until 1991, but a number of sharp-eyed incumbents already have begun plotting their survival strategies for the next decade.

The tactics vary: some House members cozy up to the state politicians responsible for drawing the lines, while other incumbents sound alarms about partisan gerrymanders, hoping to shame state legislators into not drawing them. Members who may be fiercely partisan on the House floor often lobby in their state for "sweetheart" remaps—lines that will protect incumbents of both parties. Still other members will decide that their best move for the 1990s is to move on—to a bid for higher office or into retirement.

Allies and Enemies

One way to avoid an unpleasant outcome in the line-drawing process is to build friendships with the state legislators and governors who will run the remap show in 1991. One former New York congressional aide put it this way: "As is traditional every ten years or so, an awful lot of congressmen suddenly find out what airlines fly to Al-

bany [the state capital]." New York lost five House seats after 1980 and may lose three more after the 1990 census.

In Florida, Republican members of the House delegation have a personal as well as political stake in seeing their party retain the governorship and capture the state Senate in 1990. To promote that cause, the incumbents joined with state party officials last July for a fundraiser in Orlando. "We look at it both ways: it's good for the state, it's good for the party," said GOP representative Bill McCollum. "It's good to have the governorship and the state Legislature in our hands for a lot of reasons. But if you want to look at it strictly in terms of reapportionment, it is a very important thing for us individually as well."

In Illinois, a state that may lose two seats in 1992, state Republican leaders planned to travel to Washington for a summit meeting on redistricting in the office of House Minority Leader Robert H. Michel. In Kentucky, GOP representative Jim Bunning based part of a 1989 fund-raising letter on dire redistricting speculation. In the letter, which was sent to Republicans after a report suggested the state could lose a House seat, Bunning urged supporters to "help me start my offense" and told them not to "cave in to the plots and schemes of the Frankfort Democrats who want to change our district."

The National Republican Congressional Committee (NRCC) has formally suggested some of these steps and more. At an October 6, 1989, briefing for congressional staffers, the NRCC outlined sixteen steps incumbents and delegations should take to prepare for redistricting. Among the suggestions: make contacts with state parties and legislators, get involved in state elections, gather information from the Census Bureau, and attend seminars on computerized redistricting systems.

History has shown that it is perilous for an incumbent to cross a legislator who has the power to influence redistricting. One who learned that lesson in the last round of remapping was Ohio Democratic representative Bob Shamansky. Prior to redistricting, Shamansky had angered the Democratic Speaker of the state House by endorsing a gubernatorial candidate when the Speaker himself was considering a run for the governorship. After Republicans and Democrats in the Legislature agreed to sacrifice one incumbent from each party, the House Speaker also agreed to alter Shamansky's district. Shamansky lost his bid for reelection that November.

Also in 1982 Massachusetts Democratic representative Barney Frank suffered at the hands of enemies he had made as a member of the state Legislature. The Bay State lost a seat, and legislators tried to do in Frank, who was paired with GOP representative Margaret M. Heckler in a district drawn mostly from the Republican's turf. "If you asked legislators to draw a map in which Barney Frank would never be a member of Congress again, this is it," Frank said. But he won.

Alone and Lonely

One member—Democratic representative Wayne Owens of Utah—got an early glimpse at the possible future shape of his district: it was not a pretty sight. GOP representative James V. Hansen and other Republicans circulated a remap proposal that likely would oust Owens, Utah's only Democrat in Congress. The map removed loyally Democratic territory from Owens's marginal, Salt Lake City-based district and extended his territory into more conservative rural areas.

"I'm the only Democrat in any office out there and the Republicans are having fun anticipating having at me in 1991," Owens said. Utah's redistricting process will be controlled by the GOP-dominated Legislature and by Republican governor Norman H. Bangerter. Owens lost a gubernatorial bid against Bangerter in 1984 and took over the 2d District from the GOP in 1986.

The proposed Utah map generated headlines and created some backlash that could ultimately help Owens, however. The Democratic state chairman has proposed an initiative to the state ballot that would create a bipartisan commission to handle redistricting. "I think it is safe to say [Republicans] will develop other things that will be a little less offensive," Owens said. "We are trying to argue that the urban area needs an urban congressman."

However, not all incumbents worry about arousing the wrath of state legislators. In Georgia, GOP representative Newt Gingrich, the only Republican in the state's congressional delegation, has called the leaders of the Democratic-dominated Legislature "thugs." Will that come back to haunt him at redistricting time? "They may look like donkeys, but they've got memories like elephants," state Democratic party executive director Charles Schroder said of the legislators.

The potential for a painful 1992 also may give an extra push to members of the House who are considering moving on. Every pending reapportionment brings rumors that certain members—even powerful senior ones—will choose to retire rather than deal with the headache of a reshaped constituency.

For the 1990s much speculation along these lines centers on Illinois, which has more than its share of powerful senior members, but a shrinking share of the nation's House seats. The overhaul of district lines could eliminate one seat in the Chicago area—probably a Democratic one—and another downstate—likely a Republican one. One downstate area that has lost considerable population is the central Illinois district of Minority Leader Michel, who has been in the House since 1957.

In the Chicago area, the longtime Democratic incumbents include some very influential people: Sidney R. Yates, an Appropriations subcommittee chairman first elected in 1948; Frank Annunzio, chairman of the House Administration Committee, elected in 1964; and Dan Rostenkowski, the Ways and Means chairman, who was elected in 1958. Few would expect a politician of Rostenkowski's stature to lose his seat in redistricting, but he has expressed some discontent with congressional life. He also has a $1 million campaign treasury that he could keep for personal use if he retired.

The prospect of redistricting also could increase the lure of higher office for more junior members. When Texas Democratic representative John Bryant announced that he was giving up his House seat to run for state attorney general in 1990, many speculated it was because his House district will be substantially altered by redistricting. Bryant ultimately decided to give up the statewide race and take his chances in 1992.

Affirmative Action

Although it is impossible to predict the course of redistricting in Texas, the state offers one example of the complications that can arise for incumbents even when a state is adding House seats. Texas may gain three House seats in 1992, and many consider it a foregone conclusion that one of those will be a "majority minority" district in the Dallas-Fort Worth area. The territory would be fashioned by combining minority communities that are now split between Bryant's 5th District and Democratic representative Martin Frost's 24th District.

"I think there should be a minority district and I am assuming that there will be one," said Frost, whose district is roughly one-third black and would be changed substantially by the new constituency. "There are a lot of directions my district could go in. Since I am the senior congressman from the area and I think I have a good relationship with the folks in the Legislature, I would think there'll be someplace I can run," he said.

Frost is familiar with the havoc that can be created during redistricting. By some accounts, he practically camped at the state Legislature during the last round of redistricting. At that time, many blacks allied with GOP governor William P. Clements, Jr., to push a remap that would have made Frost's district 64 percent black. That map ultimately was invalidated by federal judges. But this time around, there is strong sentiment in Democratic circles that the party cannot politically afford to anger members of the black community by resisting the creation of a majority minority district.

If some white incumbents are inconvenienced by the creation of new minority-dominated districts, even more will likely be affected by legal imperatives to preserve existing districts held by minorities. The 1982 amendments to the Voting Rights Act changed the criteria for proving racial gerrymandering. Plaintiffs once had to prove that there was an "intent" to dilute the clout of a voting bloc; now they need only prove that dilution is the "effect" of a map. Therefore, it is less likely that legislatures will eliminate any minority districts in 1992, even when they have lost a significant share of their population. That policy could lead to some unpleasant political situations for white incumbents in adjacent districts.

In Michigan the discomfort could be acute. The state may lose two seats in 1992, but no one expects the two majority-black districts in Detroit to go, even though they have suffered significant population losses. Instead, those two districts, represented by Democrats John Conyers, Jr. (1st District) and retiring George W. Crockett, Jr. (13th District), may have to reach out to surrounding districts to pick up an estimated quarter of a million people. "If you start with the assumption of two black seats in the city of Detroit," said a Michigan Democrat, "you have what I call the outward pressure problem.... The [districts of] white Democrats who surround the city of Detroit are all going to experience the pressure to come outward."

But when mapmakers look at those surrounding districts, they see a number of tough-to-budge Democratic political heavyweights. Districts near Crockett's and Conyers's include those of Rep. John D. Dingell, who is chairman of the Energy and Commerce Committee and whose son is in the state Legislature; longtime Democratic representative William D. Ford, chairman of the Post Office Committee; Democratic representative Sander M. Levin, who has a sibling in the U.S. Senate and a cousin on the state Supreme Court; Democratic representative Dennis M. Hertel, who has a brother occupying his old state House seat and another brother who may win a seat in the state Senate; and Democrat David E. Bonior, chief deputy whip in the House. If some of their districts must move outward from the Detroit area in the southeast cor-

ner of Michigan, that could put pressure on more marginal Democratic seats, including the 6th held by Rep. Bob Carr, and the 3d, held by Howard Wolpe. "There is a lot of nervous attention being paid to this right now," said one Democrat.

Sweetheart Deals

A big part of the problem in Michigan is that many Democrats are scrapping for diminishing Democratic turf. In some other areas, incumbents' redistricting worries may evaporate as both parties solidify their power by trading off unfavorable territory. These are the so-called sweetheart deals, in which, for instance, a Democrat gives up Republican constituents to a GOP district in exchange for Democratic voters, and some areas seem particularly ripe for such deals.

Florida is expected to gain three seats in 1992, and while no one can be certain where they will go, some members of the delegation already have begun making contacts with the Legislature. Some members also have talked with their House colleagues about mutually beneficial boundary changes.

On the southeast coast, Democratic representatives Harry A. Johnston, Lawrence J. Smith, and Dante B. Fascell each have a number of Republican constituents who could be moved to neighboring GOP-held districts—changes that would aid all incumbents.

The election of a Republican in Claude Pepper's Miami-based 18th District creates new opportunities for sweetheart dealing in southeast Florida. GOP representative Ileana Ros-Lehtinen would benefit from receiving Republican voters from neighboring Democratic districts, and she would be made safer by giving up Anglo voters, who overwhelmingly supported her Democratic opponent.

In Wisconsin the last round of redistricting yielded just the sort of bipartisan map that shifts lines but essentially maintains the status quo. For the most part, the map—produced by a Republican governor and Democratic legislators—kept incumbents in place. Even some very partisan figures in the state would like to see such a compromise again, and it could well happen if the current partisan split in state government lasts through the 1990 elections. One serious complication looms, however: in this round, the state may lose a seat. In that event, any number of remap scenarios are possible in a state where seven of the nine districts border at least three others.

In North Carolina Democratic legislators may try to help solidify the state's unusually high number of marginally Democratic districts. The state may gain a seat, and it may be in the best interests of Democratic incumbents for Republican voters to be taken from the marginal areas and lumped in a new GOP district. "The typical response would be the safe response and give the Republicans an extra seat or two," says North Carolina political scientist Ted Arrington. "[Democrats] can take the gutsy approach, spread themselves thinner, and risk losing several seats."

New York Intrigue

Whatever efforts incumbents make to influence line drawing, there can be no certainty in the process, only the hope of improving the odds. There may be no place of greater political intrigue than New York State, where thirty-four incumbents have a keen interest in a redistricting process that will likely eliminate three House seats.

"There is a nonpartisan issue . . . seeing that New York is not screwed in the [census] count, protecting as many seats as possible," said one Democrat. "And then there are significant partisan interests, in terms of protecting Democrats and Republicans. And then there is a significant set of personal concerns by individual members who don't want to lose their seats or be forced into an extremely expensive fight with another incumbent."

On the nonpartisan front, New Yorkers took the lead in a lawsuit aimed at forcing the Census Bureau to make statistical adjustments for an anticipated undercount of minorities in urban areas. In an out-of-court settlement during the summer of 1989, the Commerce Department, of which the Census Bureau is a part, agreed to consider the adjustment. But some New York politicians, such as Democratic representative Charles E. Schumer, say that the agreement does not settle the matter. *(Box, p. 36)*

If the 1980s redistricting process in New York is any guide, split control of state government—Democrats hold the governorship and the state Assembly, Republicans the state Senate—could lead to an even partisan split in the map drawing. In the last round, when the state lost five House seats, a new map eliminated two Democratic and two Republican districts, and created one "fair fight" district, where each party had a chance. (The GOP won that seat.)

Assuming that three seats are lost in 1990 and there is an even split, it is difficult to predict the casualties. "I've looked at a map, but you just never know what is going to be required," said GOP representative Amo Houghton, whose district is upstate. "I can't really take a scalpel or a compass or make anything of sense to it."

The conventional wisdom holds that one upstate district may go, which could mean that Houghton would be pitted against GOP representative Bill Paxon, currently in his first term. Paxon is a former state legislator, but is considered to be to the right of many in state party. Houghton, who comes from one of country's wealthiest families, was elected in 1986. He is a relative political novice, but is thought to be closer to the party mainstream than Paxon.

New York City is likely to lose at least one district, but which one remains unclear. When Brooklyn was expecting to lose a seat in 1982, many thought that Democrat Schumer, then a freshman, and Democratic representative Stephen J. Solarz would be thrown together. But Schumer, who raised more than $400,000 in preparation, and Solarz, who raised more than $700,000, ended up in safe territory. Instead, Brooklyn Democrat Leo C. Zeferetti, who had not raised nearly so much money, lost his district—even though he was one of the delegation's liaisons to the state Legislature during redistricting. A Schumer-Solarz match-up may be in the offing in 1992. But the two are no less financially prepared this time around, and some think the face-off will never happen.

Because the Legislature is unlikely to remove a minority district, speculation about other incumbent losses centers on other white members, such as longtime Democratic representative James H. Scheuer. His political career already has a nomadic quality, in part because of redistricting. Elected in 1964, Scheuer lost much of his Bronx district in 1970 when a new Hispanic district was drawn. He moved to neighboring territory and defeated fellow Democratic representative Jacob Gilbert. In 1972 Scheuer was thrown together with Democrat Jonathan Bingham when the Bronx lost a district. Scheuer lost that round, but came back in 1974, moving to and winning an open district in Brooklyn. In 1982 his district was merged with the district of Queens Democratic representative Joseph P. Addabbo, and Scheuer moved and ran successfully in the 8th District, which includes parts of Queens, the Bronx, and Nassau County.

Scheuer's irascible nature has made

him more than a few enemies, and perhaps makes him a popular target of redistricting speculation. But he has the advantage of having campaigned in many parts of the city: hardly any new district would be completely unfamiliar to him. And more important, he has the personal wealth needed to woo supporters and to discourage potential opponents.

Judicial Intervention

Adding to the uncertainty of redistricting in any state is the possibility that political factors could become secondary to legal factors. In other words, the courts may become involved in drawing the new maps. "One should go as far as humanly possible with the Legislature and with the governor," said former Scheuer aide Jonah Shacknai. "But in the final analysis, it is not at all a certainty that they will be final determinants of the legislative district boundaries."

In New York's last round of redistricting, prodding from a panel of federal judges and complaints from the Justice Department had much to do with the final map produced by the Legislature. The legal objections centered on the creation of a new Hispanic-majority district, which came at the expense of a black-majority district. The politicians went back to work, producing a modified plan that restored a black district and produced some new incumbent match-ups. It was the new map that put Scheuer in a district with Addabbo.

Amid this sort of uncertainty over district boundaries, many incumbents do whatever they can to anticipate where they could end up campaigning. One basic technique, said Shacknai, is "drawing a large circle around your existing district, and trying in ways that are inoffensive to your contiguous incumbent to get your name around and make some friends."

Montana Match-up

There is one state where line drawing is likely to be just as painful as in New York, but much more simple. Montana now appears likely to lose 50 percent of its House representation, a change that will mean simply erasing the line that separates the districts represented by Democratic representative Pat Williams and GOP representative Ron Marlenee. If population projections are accurate, the two may have no choice but to run against one another, run for something other than the House, or just stop running.

"In a humorous way, we are encouraging Montanans to have children," said a spokesman for GOP governor Stan Stephens. But in a serious way, there is not much that can be done to influence the Census Bureau count, aside from trying to make sure every last body is counted. Toward that end, the state's politicians have encouraged the bureau to expand its presence in the state to make certain all individuals are tallied. And state attorney general Mark Racicot is exploring possible legal action to block the loss of a House seat.

But if things go as currently projected, Marlenee and Williams will each be forced to assume statewide ambitions just to stay in the House in 1992. And that in turn could affect other state politicians. Williams, whom many wanted to see as a gubernatorial candidate in 1988, is weighing a bid against Stephens in 1992. He also has an eye on GOP senator Conrad Burns, who is up for reelection in 1994. Marlenee recently opted not to challenge Democratic senator Max Baucus, who is up in 1990, but could also run for governor in 1992. "There is a lot of turmoil out there right now. . . . Corks are about to pop out of the bottle in Montana," Williams said.

Part II

Outlook for the States

4

Redistricting: The Key to the House

In November 1990 voters across the United States will weigh in on the question of which party will control the House of Representatives until the twenty-first century. These decisive votes will not, however, be cast in 1990 congressional elections. They will be cast down-ballot, in contests for seats in the nation's legislatures.

In the decennial process of congressional redistricting, legislatures take the lead in shaping new boundaries. Because remapping will begin in early 1991 (using data from the 1990 census), the maps will be drawn, in the main, by legislators chosen in November 1990.

In Washington, Democratic and Republican officials tend to discuss redistricting in national and partisan terms. Democrats brag that they are a majority in two-thirds of the country's legislative chambers. Republicans tout demography, citing growth in the conservative South and West and decline in the Democratic North.

But redistricting is not a national activity, and not primarily a partisan one in many places. It is the sum of the isolated efforts of individual legislatures, carried out against the backdrop of idiosyncratic state political cultures. The drawing of lines is influenced by partisanship, to be sure, but also by ideological and regional coalitions, bipartisan alliances, personal vendettas, and

selfish ambitions within each legislature and congressional delegation. In West Virginia, for instance, remapping will be purely an intraparty feud: the Democratic governor and Democratic Legislature must shrink the all-Democratic House delegation from four to three. In Texas, Democrats control the Legislature, but a coalition of Republicans and conservative Democrats may play a leading role in drawing the new House boundaries. Ohio mapmakers of both parties threaten to knife the district of GOP representative Donald E. "Buz" Lukens if he is reelected. Lukens was convicted in May 1989 of having sex with a minor.

Redistricting is not an issue that moves the masses; it will not be a hot public topic in 1990 legislative contests. But behind the scenes, political professionals are keeping close tabs on the parties' struggle for line-drawing power. After the 1990 census, House boundaries must be redrawn in every state with more than one district. (A half-dozen states have single, at-large representatives.)

The biggest redistricting changes will occur in two places: the fast-growth states of the South and the West that are expected to gain House seats in the 1990s and the slower-growing northern states that will or may lose seats. But even states that keep their current number of House districts will

Overview of States

State (House seats)	1990 U.S. HOUSE SEAT CHANGE (Projected)	GOVERNOR (Seats up before 1991 marked *)	SENATE MAJORITY (breakdown as of 3/90)	SENATE SEATS UP IN 1990	HOUSE MAJORITY [1] (breakdown as of 3/90)
Alabama (7)	None	Guy Hunt (R) *	27-8 D	all	83-22 D
Alaska (1)	None	Open (D) *	12-8 R	half	24-16 D
Arizona (5)	+1 to +2	Open (D) *	17-13 R	all	34-26 R
Arkansas (4)	None	Bill Clinton (D) *	31-4 D	half [2]	88-11-1 D
California (45)	+4 to +6	Open (R) *	24-13-1 D (2V) †	half	46-33 D (1V)
Colorado (6)	None	Roy Romer (D) *	24-11 R	half [2]	39-26 R
Connecticut (6)	None	Open (D) *	23-13 D	all	88-63 D
Delaware (1)	None	Michael N. Castle (R)	13-8 D	half [2]	23-18 R
Florida (19)	+3	Bob Martinez (R) *	23-17 D	half	72-48 D
Georgia (10)	+1 to +2	Open (D) *	45-11 D	all	144-36 D
Hawaii (2)	None	John Waihee III (D) *	22-3 D	half [2]	45-6 D
Idaho (2)	None	Cecil D. Andrus (D) *	24-18 R	all	63-21 R
Illinois (22)	-2	Open (R) *	31-28 D	one-third [3]	67-51 D
Indiana (10)	None	Evan Bayh (D)	26-24 R	half	51-49 R
Iowa (6)	-1	Terry E. Branstad (R) *	30-20 D	half	61-39 D
Kansas (5)	-1	Mike Hayden (R) *	22-18 R	none	68-57 R
Kentucky (7)	None	Wallace G. Wilkinson (D)	30-8 D	half	71-29 D
Louisiana (8)	None	Buddy Roemer (D)	33-6 D	none	86-18-1 D
Maine (2)	None	John R. McKernan, Jr. (R) *	20-15 D	all	98-53 D
Maryland (8)	None	William Donald Schaefer (D) *	40-7 D	all	125-16 D
Massachusetts (11)	0 to -1	Open (D) *	32-8 D	all	128-32 D
Michigan (18)	-2	James J. Blanchard (D) *	20-18 R	all	60-50 D

State	Net change	Governor	Seats up	Senate	House
Minnesota (8)	None	Rudy Perpich (D) *	all	44-23 D	80-54 D
Mississippi (5)	None	Ray Mabus (D)	none	43-9 D	105-17 D
Missouri (9)	None	John Ashcroft (R)	half	23-10 D (1V)	104-59 D
Montana (2)	0 to −1	Stan Stephens (R)	half	27-23 R	52-48 D
Nebraska (3)	None	Kay A. Orr (R) *	half[2]	—[4]	—[4]
Nevada (2)	None	Bob Miller (D) *	half[2]	13-8 R	30-12 D
New Hampshire (2)	None	Judd Gregg (R) *	all	16-8 R	275-119-1 R (5V)
New Jersey (14)	None	Jim Florio (D)	none	23-17 D	44-36 R
New Mexico (3)	None	Open (R) *	none	25-17 D	45-25 D
New York (34)	−2 to −3	Mario M. Cuomo (D) *	all	34-27 R	92-58 D
North Carolina (11)	0 to +1	James G. Martin (R)	all	38-12 D	74-46 D
North Dakota (1)	None	George Sinner (D)	half[2]	32-21 D	61-45 R
Ohio (21)	−2	Open (D) *	half[2]	19-14 R	59-40 D
Oklahoma (6)	None	Open (R) *	half	33-15 D	69-32 D
Oregon (5)	None	Open (D) *	half	19-11 D	32-28 D
Pennsylvania (23)	−2 to −3	Robert P. Casey (D) *	half	27-22 R (1V)	102-99 D (2V)
Rhode Island (2)	None	Edward D. DiPrete (R) *	all	41-9 D	86-14 D
South Carolina (6)	None	Carroll A. Campbell, Jr. (R) *	none	35-11 D	82-42 D
South Dakota (1)	None	George S. Mickelson (R) *	all	20-15 R	46-24 R
Tennessee (9)	None	Ned McWherter (D) *	half[2]	22-11 D	59-40 D
Texas (27)	+3 to +4	Open (R) *	half[2]	23-8 D	90-60 D
Utah (3)	None	Norman H. Bangerter (R)	half[2]	22-7 R	48-27 R
Vermont (1)	None	Open (D) *	all	16-14 D	75-75
Virginia (10)	0 to +1	L. Douglas Wilder (D)	none	30-10 D	59-39-2 D
Washington (8)	None	Booth Gardner (D)	half[2]	25-24 R	63-35 D
West Virginia (4)	−1	Gaston Caperton (D)	half	30-4 D	80-20 D
Wisconsin (9)	0 to −1	Tommy G. Thompson (R) *	half[2]	19-14 D	55-42 D (2V)
Wyoming (1)	None	Mike Sullivan (D) *	half	19-11 R	41-23 R

† "V" stands for vacancy.

[1] All state House members are up in 1990 in every state except Louisiana, Mississippi, New Jersey, and Virginia, which have odd-year state legislative elections.

[2] These states have an odd number of Senate seats; therefore, one more or one less than half the seats are up.

[3] Under its staggered-term system, Illinois will elect twenty of its fifty-nine state senators in 1990.

[4] Nebraska has a forty-nine-seat nonpartisan unicameral Legislature.

have to adjust district lines to account for intrastate population imbalances that have developed during the 1980s.

In forty of the forty-four congressional redistricting states, the legislatures have primary responsibility for redrawing district lines. Even in Iowa and Washington state, where state commissions or agencies are established to draw the maps, the legislatures will have a final say on the plan. Only Hawaii and Montana exclude their legislatures from the process. So for the most part, the party that dominates a legislature after next year's elections will have a firm first hand on the "redistricting pen."

Partisanship has been one of the driving forces behind redistricting for many years—even before the birth of the "gerrymander." Officials of both parties are pointing to the 1990 legislative elections as crucial in enhancing their opportunities to take advantage of redistricting. But 1990's races are actually the last in a series of skirmishes during the 1980s that have cost the national parties millions of dollars in campaign contributions and technical assistance to targeted legislative campaigns.

The first volley in this national battle for legislative control was fired early in the 1980s when the GOP unveiled its "1991 Plan"; the goal is to overturn the traditional Democratic tilt at the legislative level. But the national Democratic party responded with "Project 500," which aimed to capture or maintain control of 500 legislative seats in time for the next remap. Going into the 1989-1990 elections, Democrats controlled both houses in twenty-seven of the forty-two legislatures that perform congressional redistricting; in seven other states, Democrats have a majority in one house and thus a say in the remap process. Republicans dominate the legislatures in just eight of the forty-two states. Majority control of a legislature can indeed enable a party to reap significant benefits. In California's last redistricting,

the remap, crafted by the late Democratic representative Phillip Burton, gave Democrats a huge boost in House seats. *(Burton remap, p. 93)*

But partisan control does not guarantee the outcome of redistricting. In 1981 the Republicans who then controlled the Indiana Legislature drafted a map designed to give them a windfall of House seats. But Democrats were able to hold the Republicans in 1982 to a 5-5 House seat split, and since then the GOP has slipped to a 3-7 deficit.

Partisan control also does not necessarily translate into partisan bloodlust. In Kentucky, for example, the dominant Democrats crafted a plan for the 1980s that left in place a four-Democrat/three-Republican division that prevails. In Florida, Texas, and Nevada, Democrats in the late 1970s had strong majorities, but in each of these states, a coalition of conservative Democrats and Republicans backed plans that benefited the GOP.

Moreover, partisanship sometimes takes a back seat to personal and parochial influences in redistricting. In Pennsylvania, a Republican effort to craft a safe GOP district near Philadelphia was blocked by members of a bipartisan local coalition who did not want their county divided between congressional districts. One of the flaws in the Indiana "gerrymander" was that Republican legislators took GOP voters from surrounding areas and packed them into a single suburban Indianapolis district; the aim was to benefit state GOP official Bruce Melchert, but he lost in his House primary.

Redistricting also lends insight into a state's politics. In Illinois, remapping is fiercely partisan; the Democratic plan for the 1980s merged four suburban Republican districts into two, while preserving all the Democratic districts in Chicago. But across the Mississippi River in Iowa, a state with strong "reform" tendencies, the Legislature defers responsibility for redrawing the lines to its nonpartisan bill-drafting agency.

Legislatures do not, of course, have total control over redistricting. In most states, the governor can veto remap plans; therefore, the thirty-six gubernatorial elections held during 1990 will have a strong bearing on redistricting. In addition, the federal courts play a significant role in redistricting. In the last round of line-drawing, courts ordered changes in several congressional maps, finding in favor of the "out" political party or a racial or ethnic minority group that said its rights had been violated by a gerrymandered remap. Sixteen states must obtain U.S. Justice Department approval of their redistricting plans under the Voting Rights Act.

Still, it is the legislatures that begin, set the tone for, and often dominate redistricting. The partisan composition of the legislatures and their peculiar personalities will decisively shape the Democratic-Republican division in the U.S. House during the 1990s.

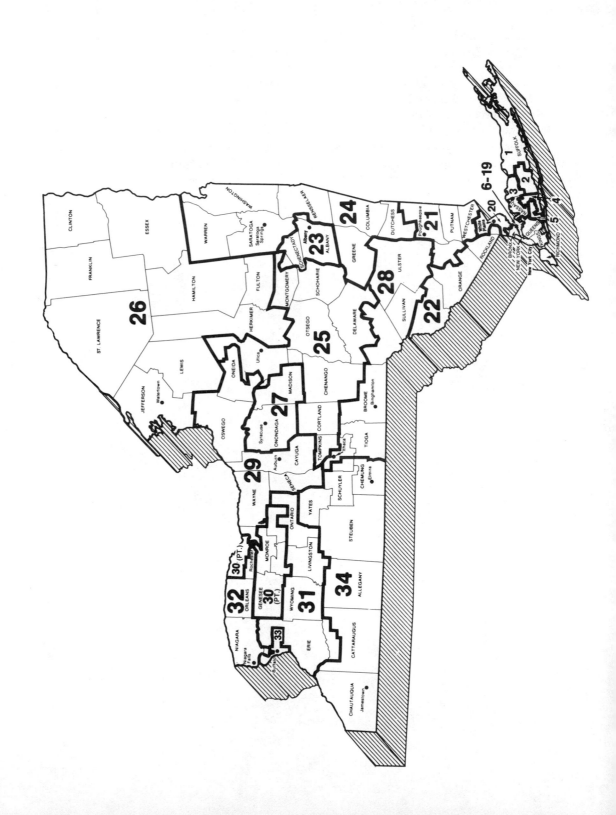

5

States Losing Seats

New York

Population and growth

1980 population	17,558,072
1989 population estimate	17,950,000
(2d in the nation)	
Percent change 1980-1989	+2%

U.S. Congress

Senate	1 D,	1 R
House	21 D,	13 R

State legislature

Senate	27 D,	34 R
House	92 D,	58 R
Governor	Mario M. Cuomo, D	

Once again, New York's Legislature will face the unwelcome task of redrawing the congressional district map to compensate for a loss of seats. Redistricting analysts project that New York, whose estimated population increased by a little more than 2 percent between 1980 and 1989, will likely lose three House seats after the 1990 census.

This loss is not as severe as the five-seat loss after 1980, but, if the projections hold up, it will mark the fifth consecutive decade that New York has suffered a multiple-seat loss. From forty-five House seats in the

1940s (the same number California currently has), New York could fall to thirty-one.

To try to limit the damage, New York's state and federal officials are battling to get what they see as their fair share of seats. Convinced that the Census Bureau failed to count thousands of black and Hispanic residents in 1980, New York officials have been actively involved in efforts to force the bureau to adjust its 1990 enumeration to compensate for another expected minority undercount. "It is absolutely scandalous that these people would not be counted in a census," said Democratic representative Eliot L. Engel. New York is also fighting efforts by states with few illegal aliens to end the inclusion of that population in the census count.

Still, the loss of House seats is almost an inevitability, and the pain is likely to be bipartisan. Democrats hold an indomitable 92-58 majority in the state Assembly; Republicans have a smaller but time-tested edge in the state Senate (34-27). Democratic governor Mario M. Cuomo, who has veto power over the redistricting plan, will be a strong favorite if he decides to seek reelection in 1990.

In the last round of redistricting, when a similar split prevailed, the Legislature divided the damage evenly. Two Republican districts in the Syracuse area were merged, as were two GOP-held seats on Long Island. But the Republicans ultimately gained a slight edge, thanks to the merger of two Democratic districts in the Bronx and the creation of two districts in which a GOP incumbent had an advantage over a Democratic colleague (Guy V. Molinari over Leo C. Zeferetti in New York City, and Benjamin A. Gilman over Peter A. Peyser in the city's outer suburbs and exurbs).

A similar compromise after 1990 probably would result in the removal of one Democratic seat in the New York City area and a Republican seat in western New York. Should the state lose three seats, a "fair fight" district might be created, perhaps in metropolitan New York City or in the Albany/central New York regions.

But while a "macro" level compromise may be fairly easy to envision, the "micro" decisions that can end incumbents' careers will be much more difficult. Complicating matters is the fact that many of the districts that have lost population—such as the heavily black 11th and 16th and the Hispanic-and-black 18th—are served by minority-group members certain to be held harmless in redistricting, due to the exigencies of the Voting Rights Act.

The cuts will thus have to come from the remaining handful of districts, many of them held by incumbents not at all shy about jockeying for a secure position in redistricting. For example, eight-term Democratic representative Stephen J. Solarz, who used his prolific fund-raising ability as a shield in the last round, has a campaign reserve of more than $1 million.

Even less senior members appear to have some sort of cushion. Engel, a six-term member of the state Assembly before his 1988 election to the 19th District (South Yonkers; East and Central Bronx), thinks his constituency should survive remapping

relatively intact; it had an estimated 6 percent population growth through 1986. But he adds that he will "make my case with the people I know" if he faces any redistricting difficulties.

Engel will not be alone at the Legislature's door. Democratic state representative Angelo Del Toro noted that most of the state's congressional delegation was in Albany in the summer of 1989 for a reception staged by Assembly Speaker Melvin H. Miller. "Some of these guys we haven't seen for a long time," Del Toro said wryly. "Maybe I'm just suspicious."

Looking to 1990, New York politicos are focusing on the contest for the state Senate, where all the seats are up in November and there is more prospect of a switch in party control than in the Assembly. A partisan switch, however, is still very much a long shot. The split Legislature in the early 1980s also produced a "sweetheart" deal on state legislative redistricting: the GOP majority in the Senate and the Democrats in the House designed their own districts.

Along with this structural advantage of incumbency, the GOP majority is backed by the formidable fund-raising and targeting efforts of the Republican Senate Campaign Committee (RSCC). According to state senator Guy Velella, the Bronx Republican who chairs the RSCC, the committee raised $2 million for the 1988 elections and "will spend whatever is necessary to win" in 1990. Despite the Republicans' long-term hold on the Senate, Velella said, the GOP can leave nothing to chance. "If the Democrats gained control, a lot of Republican legislators will be running from the Canadian border down to Brooklyn," he said.

On the minority side, Democratic Senate Campaign Committee chairman Anthony M. Masiello said his organization hopes to raise $1 million for 1990 and started its recruiting for targeted districts earlier than ever. But many other Democrats are not brimming with optimism. "Being a Democrat, I hope it happens, but it's awfully hard to beat incumbents," Engel said.

Whatever New York has to do following the 1990 census, it is well equipped to do it. New York is the only state with a permanent Legislative Task Force on Demographic Research and Reapportionment, a New York City-based arm of the Legislature. While most other states were still shopping computer vendor fairs for redistricting hardware and software in the summer of 1989, the task force's twenty-member technical staff was already digitizing election district maps and punching in election results to create a database for the high-tech redistricting of the 1990s.

The task force was set up as a temporary committee to handle the 1980s redistricting. But according to Executive Director Thomas W. Wallace of the New York State Board of Elections, the Legislature saw the need to maintain it as an ongoing enterprise.

The task force also provides a forum for Democrats and Republicans to negotiate the compromises that have been—and may continue to be—mandated by the divided partisan control of the Legislature. The task force is headed by a committee made up of three members from each party, including the co-chairmen, Senate Republican Dean G. Skelos and Assembly Democrat David F. Gantt.

The New York task force should not be confused with the nonpartisan, apolitical legislative service bodies that assist in redistricting in states such as Iowa and Washington. The members of the New York committee get their guidance from the caucus leaders and individual legislators. The partisan division in the Legislature means much of this input is oriented toward protecting incumbents rather than toward seeking partisan advantage, but the work is still very political.

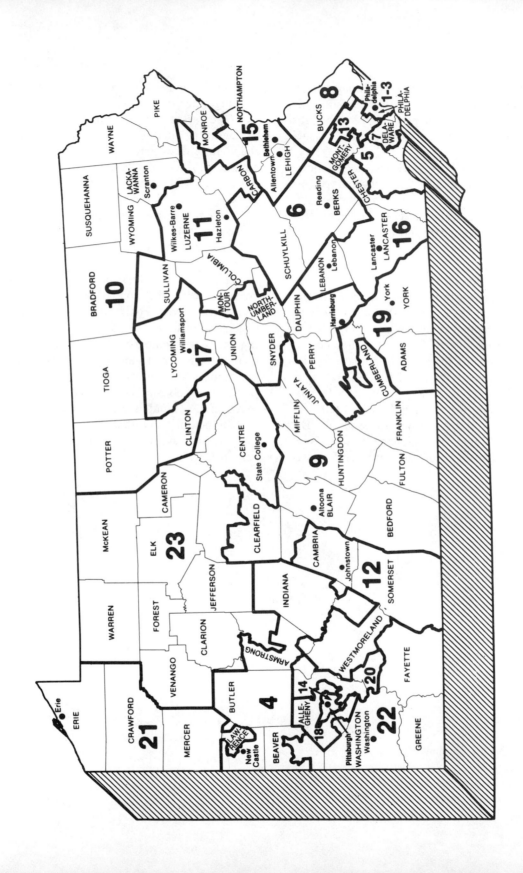

Pennsylvania

Population and growth

1980 population	11,863,895
1989 population estimate	12,040,000
(5th in the nation)	
Percent change 1980-1989	+1%

U.S. Congress

Senate 2 R
House 12 D, 11 R

State legislature

Senate 22 D, 27 R, 1 Vacancy
House 102 D, 99 R, 2 Vacancies
Governor Robert P. Casey, D

In few states are the redistricting stakes higher and the legislative balance more delicate than in Pennsylvania. With its population remaining stagnant due to the decline in steel, coal, and other heavy industries, Pennsylvania—which lost two House seats after the 1980 census—is likely to lose two or three more in the 1990s. And as the state approaches this painful redistricting, its Legislature is divided right down the middle: Republicans hold a 27-22 majority in the state Senate, while Democrats have a 102-99 edge in the state House.

The track record of recent legislative elections indicates that gains in 1990 by either party in either house will be extremely hard won. The current narrow margins held by the GOP in the Senate and Democrats in the House have been roughly frozen since the 1982 elections.

There is good reason for this stability. Unlike congressional redistricting—which follows the normal legislative process and is responsive to whichever party has a majority—state legislative redistricting in Pennsylvania is handled by a commission composed of the Democratic and Republican caucus leaders in the state Senate and House, plus one nonpartisan member. After the last census, the commission produced a balanced plan with plenty of safe districts.

Added to these structural advantages are incumbent benefits similar to those enjoyed by members of Congress. "The Legislature is a full-time body, with the perks of office such as an office budget, staff, newsletters," said Lowman Henry, executive director of the Pennsylvania Republican party in July 1989. "It makes it difficult for a challenger."

In the 1988 state House elections, for example, only 7 of the 203 state House seats switched parties, with Democrats winning 4 and Republicans 3. Even this minimal turnover was the first net gain for either party since 1982, when the Democrats netted 3 seats and regained control, 103-100. In 1988 only eleven state House candidates—eight Democrats and three Republicans—won with less than 55 percent of the vote. Seventy-one candidates ran without major party opposition.

State Republicans, with a major assist from national party campaign committees, put on a full-court press in a May 1989 special state House election in Armstrong County, a swing-voting blue-collar area northeast of Pittsburgh. Combined spending on behalf of GOP candidate James Scahill ran to about $100,000, more than double the average spent on a competitive state House race in 1988. Democrat Tim Pesci beat Scahill by 737 votes.

The urgency of the Republican effort to win the House, and especially to hold the Senate (half the seats are up in 1990), is magnified by the fact that Democratic governor Robert P. Casey is favored for reelection. A Casey win and a Democratic capture of the Senate would reverse the situation that prevailed in 1981, when the governor was Republican Dick Thornburgh and the GOP had narrow majorities in both houses.

Republican mapmakers then did manage to eliminate two Democratic seats, one in Philadelphia and one in the western part of the state. But regional rivalries tempered more ambitious Republican line-drawing attempts. Efforts were made, for example, to craft a safe GOP district by taking parts of affluent but politically marginal Bucks County and merging them with parts of affluent, Republican Montgomery County. But this plan was blocked by legislators and local political activists waging a campaign to "keep Bucks County whole." In the 1982 election after redistricting, Democrat Peter H. Kostmayer, who had lost the Bucks County seat in 1980, defeated Republican incumbent James K. Coyne.

This willingness by legislators to cross party lines in behalf of regional or personal interests—combined with the extremely close division in both legislative houses—militates against an obvious gerrymander. "It would be tough to ramrod through anything that is too tilted to one side," said the GOP's Henry. "It is very unlikely that you would see a California-type plan in Pennsylvania."

Henry maintains that population trends, including a continued population decline in several heavily Democratic areas in western Pennsylvania and parts of Philadelphia and a modest increase in some GOP suburbs and exurbs, mandate a reapportionment "fair" to Republicans. But the Democrats, who are almost certain to have a role in the process, will surely insist it is unfair that all of the state's loss of seats come in their areas of strength.

Michigan

Population and growth

1980 population	9,262,078
1989 population estimate	9,273,000
(8th in the nation)	
Percent change 1980-1989	0%

U.S. Congress

Senate 2 D
House 11 D, 7 R

State legislature

Senate 18 D, 20 R
House 60 D, 50 R
Governor James J. Blanchard, D

The population decline brought on by Michigan's recession in the early 1980s appears over; Census Bureau estimates show that Michigan had almost exactly as many people in 1989 as in 1980. Nonetheless, Michigan has been left in the dust by the faster growing Sunbelt states, and is likely to lose two House seats after 1990.

Republicans thus hardly have to be reminded of the importance of holding their state Senate majority, a narrow 20-18. With Democratic governor James J. Blanchard looking strong entering his 1990 campaign for a third term and his party holding a comfortable 60-50 edge in the state House, only the Republican Senate stands in the way of Democratic control of the redistricting process.

A similar situation prevailed during the last state Senate elections in 1986, when Republicans defended the 20-18 majority they had captured because of a full-blown tax revolt. In 1983, his first year as governor, Blanchard pushed a huge temporary income-tax surcharge through the Legislature to redress a recession-swelled state deficit. A furious reaction by anti-tax groups in the Macomb and Oakland County

suburbs north of Detroit resulted in the recalls of Democratic senators Philip O. Mastin and David M. Serotkin, who had voted for the tax hike.

In special elections held in February 1984, Republican candidates captured the two "recall districts" and gave the GOP its slim majority. These districts topped the Democrats' target list in 1986, but the Republicans held on to them—even as Blanchard, his popularity revived, scored a landslide reelection.

Many Michigan politicos credit the party's 1986 success to the GOP Senate caucus' strong campaign organization. At a dinner in May 1989—a year and a half before the next legislative elections—the Senate campaign committee raised more than $500,000, en route to a goal of $1.7 million for 1990 (when all the Senate seats are up). While much of this money is used to secure GOP-held seats, some is channeled into challenger races. On the House side, it is the Democratic caucus that has the stronger campaign organization.

Though control of the Legislature has been the subject of partisan contention throughout the 1980s, party activists doubt it has much appeal as a voting issue. "We're going to be doing some questioning to find out whether it's an issue the electorate will find understandable or interesting," said Carol Norris, Michigan Democratic party executive director in August 1989. "We're not sure it will work."

However, political strategists say the issue of partisan control does have utility among activists. "It will be the driving issue in respect to our ability to raise money," said Saul Anuzis, executive assistant to GOP state senator Dick Posthumus, the assistant majority leader. "This state being labor-dominated when [the Democrats] govern the state raises fear within the business community."

When legislators sit down to draw new

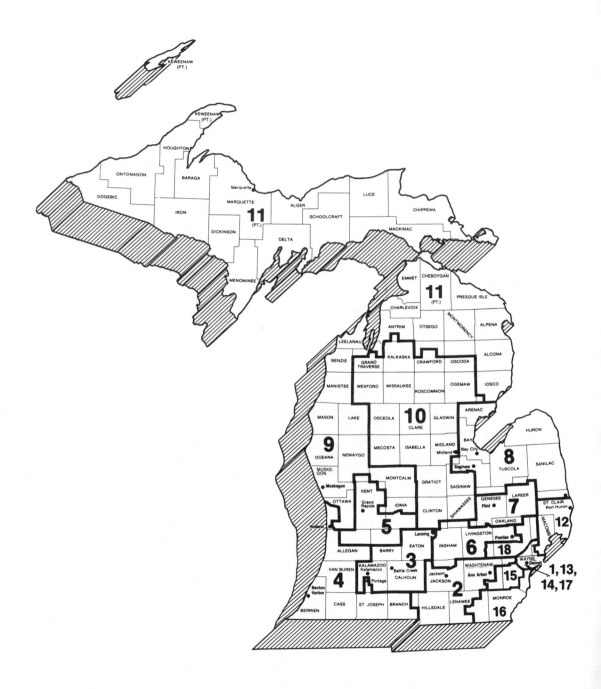

congressional lines for the 1990s, they will find that most of the districts that have lost people are held by Democrats. For example, George W. Crockett, Jr.'s 13th District in inner-city Detroit lost an estimated 14 percent of its population between 1980 and 1986, the biggest decline in the nation. The only Michigan districts to gain appreciably in population are Republican-held: Paul B. Henry's 5th in Grand Rapids and William S. Broomfield's 18th in suburban Detroit.

"I don't see how they could get a Republican," said Tom Shields, president of Lansing's Marketing Resource Group and a leading GOP consultant. But anything could happen if Democrats gain full control of the Legislature, as they had during the last redistricting. Shields said that when he was told last time that the 6th, a compact, Lansing-based district, was being reconfigured to reach from Democrat-leaning East Lansing to blue-collar Pontiac

sixty miles away, "I laughed." But a map containing the district passed the Legislature and was upheld by a federal court panel after a veto by GOP governor William G. Milliken.

Even reaching a compromise to eliminate one seat per party will be difficult. It is nearly certain that, despite the population falloff in inner-city Detroit, a strong effort will be made to preserve the city's two majority-black districts by extending them into the suburbs. But in every direction around the city is a Democratic incumbent with a high position or impressive political ties. They include John D. Dingell, chairman of the Energy and Commerce Committee; William D. Ford, chairman of the Post Office and Civil Service Committee; David E. Bonior, chief deputy whip; Dennis M. Hertel, a member of a prominent local political family, and Sander M. Levin, brother of Sen. Carl Levin.

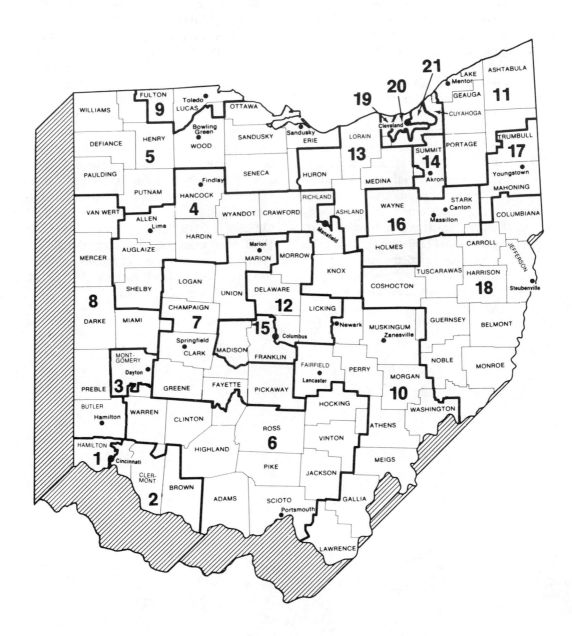

Ohio

Population and growth

1980 population	10,797,630
1989 population estimate	10,907,000
(7th in the nation)	
Percent change 1980-1989	+1%

U.S. Congress

Senate	2 D
House	11 D, 10 R

State legislature

Senate	14 D, 19 R
House	59 D, 40 R
Governor	Richard F. Celeste, D

The post-1990 redistricting outlook in Ohio mirrors the situation that existed after the 1980 count. With the agonies of its heavy industrial sector stifling population growth, Ohio is again expected to lose two House seats. And as in the last round, the remap is expected to be handled by a split Legislature: Republicans hold a 19-14 majority in the state Senate, while Democrats maintain a sturdy 59-40 margin in the state House of Representatives.

Few in either party expect this situation to change in the 1990 elections, in which half the Senate seats and all in the House will be contested. The GOP's ability to hold its Senate majority is widely credited to its caucus campaign organization, constructed and steered by strategist Jim Tilling, who doubles as chief administrative officer for the Senate. Despite a 1988 Democratic thrust that targeted four Republican seats, the GOP ended up gaining a seat, upsetting a Democratic incumbent.

In the House, however, the Republican minority has been stymied by the prolific fund raising of Speaker Vern G. Riffe, Jr.; the GOP's seat total is the most it has held since the last legislative remapping.

The similar split after 1980 resulted in a congressional remap that eliminated one Democratic and one Republican seat. In 1990 the largest population declines appear to be in industrial northeastern Ohio cities such as Cleveland and Youngstown, and some Republicans maintain that the two-seat loss should be totally absorbed in this heavily Democratic region. "We will fight the Democrats tooth and nail if they try to take a Republican seat," said Ohio GOP Executive Director Brian Berry.

However, Tilling, who also is responsible for developing policy for the Republican caucus, takes a pragmatic view. Noting that he participated in negotiations with a Democratic state House consultant that led to the last round's compromise plan, Tilling said he "would expect the same situation" this time.

Which members would face the redistricting knife under such a plan? With Cleveland Democrats Louis Stokes (Ohio's only black House member) and Mary Rose Oakar (one of two women in the delegation) seemingly untouchable, the fate of Democratic representative Edward F. Feighan—whose U-shaped, suburban 19th District surrounds the city—has been the subject of much speculation.

But Feighan, in his fifth term, has many friends in the Cuyahoga County Democratic leadership and in the state House, where he served three terms in the 1970s. Another possible target is maverick Youngstown Democrat James A. Traficant, Jr. (17th District). He has been embroiled in a protracted legal battle over back taxes the Internal Revenue Service says he owes on bribes he is alleged to have accepted as Mahoning County sheriff. (Traficant was acquitted on federal criminal charges involving the same allegations.)

If the GOP must sacrifice a seat, it is likely to be in the western part of the state. The heavily Republican 7th District will have a freshman member when the map is redrawn. Republican representative Mike DeWine is giving that seat up to run for lieutenant governor.

The neighboring 8th District may also have a new face in the House: although Republican representative Donald E. "Buz" Lukens filed to run for reelection, his political future was on hold as he appealed his 1989 conviction on misdemeanor charges of having sex with a sixteen-year-old girl. In the meantime, former GOP representative Thomas N. Kindness and state representative John Boehner staged an active campaign for the May 1990 primary in the 8th District.

The Republican delegation also has two members—Chalmers P. Wylie (15th District) and Clarence E. Miller (10th District)—who will be over seventy years old in 1990. But neither member has hinted at retirement.

Illinois

Population and growth

1980 population	11,426,518
1989 population estimate	11,658,000
(6th in the nation)	
Percent change 1980-1989	+2%

U.S. Congress

Senate	2 D
House	14 D, 8 R

State legislature

Senate	31 D, 28 R
House	67 D, 51 R
Governor	James R. Thompson, R

The census is likely to bring bad news to Illinois again. With its population increasing minimally during the 1980s, the state faces the loss of two House seats for the second consecutive decade. A fall to twenty seats would give Illinois its lowest level of House representation since the 1880s.

Even with the shrinkage, state Republicans maintain that any fair redrawing will improve their position in a House delegation in which they are now an 8-14 minority. The GOP sees it as a given that at least one of the lost seats should come from Democratic Chicago. But Republicans also say the entire Chicago region should be redrawn to reflect population trends: the state's only districts to grow by more than 5 percent between 1980 and 1986 were the suburban, GOP-held 10th, 12th, 13th, and 14th. The Chicago-based 1st, 3d, 7th, and 9th—all Democratic—lost people.

A 1980s population loss in excess of 30,000 people in the west-central 18th District—brought on by a recession in Peoria's industrial economy—would appear to place at risk House Minority Leader Robert H. Michel. However, the neighboring 17th

(Rock Island; Moline), served by four-term Democrat Lane Evans, has similarly declined.

Any Republican effort to make lemonade out of the lemon of losing a seat will be counterbalanced by the fact that Democrats are all but assured a role in the next redistricting; in fact, in the 1990 elections, they will be taking a run at complete control of the process. Already endowed with an iron 67-51 majority in the state House, Democrats will aim to protect a 31-28 state Senate edge that is tenuous but has withstood a series of GOP challenges. Further, the retirement of Republican governor James R. Thompson gives Democrats an even chance of winning the third leg in the redistricting triad; the race between Democratic state attorney general Neil F. Hartigan and Republican secretary of state Jim Edgar to succeed Thompson is expected to be close.

Trepidation over the prospect of Democratic control of redistricting ought to provide an adrenaline boost to Republican campaign efforts next year. The Democrats exhibited a ruthless skill at redistricting during the last remap.

Ironically, Republicans appeared to hold the upper hand when that process began after the 1980 elections. While Democrats had a slim majority in the state Senate, Republicans held the governorship and the state House. With the 2-1 Republican majority on the federal district court as insurance in the event of a stalemate, the GOP seemed at least assured of a compromise redistricting plan.

But the Democrats decided to play hardball by blocking legislative proposals and taking their chances with the federal court. There they had the benefit of a secret weapon: the expertise of political consultant Kimball W. Brace, then a pioneer in the use of computers for redistricting, who had been brought in by state House Democratic

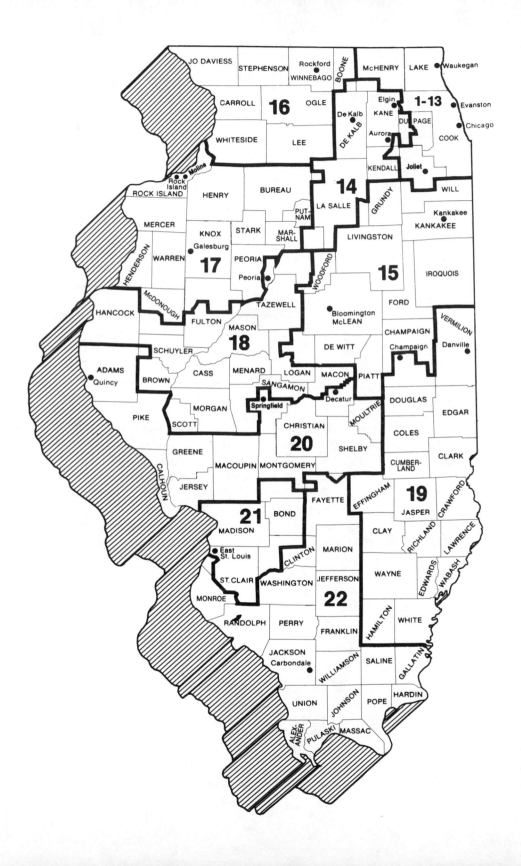

leader Michael J. Madigan. Brace's Election Data Services in Washington, D.C., devised innovative programs that not only crafted districts of unstinting population equality, but also exposed miscalculations and inaccuracies in the Republican-proposed plans.

Despite the Republican majority on the bench, the court accepted the Madigan-Brace plan, with its strongly Democratic orientation. The plan merged four Republican districts in the Chicago suburbs into two (costing GOP representatives Robert McClory and Edward J. Derwinski their seats). It preserved all the Democratic districts in Chicago by radiating them, as slightly as possible, into the suburbs, in the process preserving three districts with overwhelming black majorities. In addition, three downstate Republican districts, drawn to be competitive, were later taken over by Democrats.

The Democrats also sold a heavily self-oriented redistricting plan for the state Legislature to a special nine-member commission. Along with their map-making skill, the Democrats needed a lot of luck in this coup. The tie-breaking vote on the commission was cast by former Democratic governor Samuel H. Shapiro, who was selected for the panel by an "only in Illinois" procedure: his name was picked out of a hat that also contained a slip with the name of a prominent Republican. In another unique touch, the hat, borrowed from a state museum, once belonged to Abraham Lincoln.

The state remap helped the Democrats gain and hold control of the Legislature through the 1980s. For the Senate, the chief result of the last remap was to create large numbers of safe districts; although incumbents in both parties have benefited, the map has helped Democrats hang on to their narrow majority. Despite big-spending campaigns by both parties, all thirty-nine senators up in 1988 won reelection. "It comes

down to the map," said Deb Detmers, assistant to the chief executive of the Senate Republican Caucus in August 1989. "There are very few competitive seats."

The effects of the last redistricting on the state House were immediate and dramatic. In the first election after the remap—which coincided with a massive reorganization that reduced the membership of the state House—Madigan's Democrats went from an 86-91 minority to a 70-48 majority. Although the Reagan landslide helped the Republicans recoup three seats in 1984, the Democrats have been able to hold at 67-51 through the last two elections.

The Democratic advantages of redistricting and incumbency are bolstered by the fund raising and targeting of House Speaker Madigan's campaign organization. Each of the Legislature's other caucuses has a well-oiled campaign machine, but Madigan is the acknowledged master. Madigan's House Democratic Majority Committee takes in about $2 million per campaign cycle and provides party candidates with cash contributions, staff, radio and TV ads, and advice from hired consultants and pollsters. According to Madigan's chief of staff, Gary LaPaille, the Democratic leadership fund, which collected a total of about $50,000 per campaign year when Madigan took over, now contributes that much to individual candidates. In addition, Madigan kicks in about $500,000 in transfers from his own campaign fund, the Friends of Madigan Committee.

In the face of these odds, Republicans point to some limited advances, including gains among conservative ethnics in and near Chicago; their wariness of national Democratic liberalism was exacerbated by the control of Chicago's City Hall by black Democrats in the mid-1980s. In the 7th Senate District, which straddles the border of northwest Chicago and the suburbs, Republican senator Walter W. Dudycz won a second term in 1988 by a 2-1 margin. (Dudycz is challenging veteran Democratic U.S. representative Frank Annunzio in 1990 in the 11th Congressional District.) In the 47th House District, located just west of Chicago, Republican Ann Zickus won 52 percent of the vote in 1988 to unseat Democratic incumbent John T. O'Connell. In the neighboring 48th, which reaches into the city, Democratic representative Robert M. Terzich held off Republican Wayne M. Straza by just 197 votes.

But also in 1988, the GOP suffered a setback in southeast Chicago's 35th District: Republican representative Samuel Panayotovich, a recent party-switcher, lost to Democrat Clement Balanoff by nearly 10 percentage points. Elected to a third state House term in 1986 as a Democrat, Panayotovich then joined with his local ally Edward Vrdolyak, former Cook County Democratic party chairman, in jumping to the GOP.

The move made Panayotovich a symbol of Republican efforts to realign Chicago, but it also made him a target of Madigan's formidable campaign organization. "We went after him," LaPaille said, "to show that you can't be a turncoat and get a free pass."

Iowa

Population and growth

1980 population	2,913,808
1989 population estimate	2,840,000
(29th in the nation)	
Percent change 1980-1989	-3%

U.S. Congress

Senate	1 D,	1 R
House	2 D,	4 R

State legislature

Senate	30 D,	20 R
House	61 D,	39 R
Governor	Terry E. Branstad, R	

Population decline, brought on by economic difficulties in Iowa's farm and industrial sectors, is likely to cost the state a House seat after the 1990 census. And because population has dropped in every district except the Des Moines-based 4th (according to 1980-1986 estimates), virtually anyone in the delegation of four Republicans and two Democrats is vulnerable to being paired.

Although the partisan stakes are plainly high, Iowa's district map will again be drawn by a nonpartisan agency of the state Legislature. The 1990s round of redistricting marks the second since the Iowa Legislature (then GOP-controlled) passed a law in 1980 authorizing its Legislative Services Bureau, a nonpartisan bill-drafting division, to draw the district maps. Reflecting the state's proclivities for "squeaky clean" government, the legislators aimed to limit the role of partisanship in redistricting after the 1980 census. They succeeded to a large degree, but also proved just how hard it is to remove politics entirely from the very political business of line-drawing.

As the law envisioned it, the bureau's efforts would be thoroughly divorced from politics. Neither legislators nor outsiders were provided access to the deliberations of bureau technicians. The law mandated that the bureau follow apolitical criteria—such as district population equality and compactness—in drawing the lines. It forbade the map makers from using data such as party registration and even barred them from acting to prevent the pairing of incumbents by factoring in their home addresses.

However, the legislators gave themselves a say in the process: if they rejected the bureau's first three proposals, they would get to draw the district map themselves. As it turned out, the goals of the law ran smack into the legislators' partisan instincts. When the bureau presented a map that paired Republican representatives Jim Leach and Tom Tauke, GOP leaders blasted the plan as more Democratic than even the Democrats would have dared draw. "All at once, we knew where [the incumbents] lived," quipped Legislative Services Bureau legal counsel Gary L. Kaufman.

By 21-28 the state Senate rejected the plan in May 1981. Because the bureau could not be blamed for following its mandate to ignore political criteria, the Republican majority based its decision on population inequality—even though the average district deviation from the "ideal" population size was only 0.0392 percent. The bureau returned in June with a plan that had an even smaller population variance; it separated Tauke and Leach and met with the approval of GOP governor Robert D. Ray. However, Republican state senators viewed the inclusion of Democratic-leaning Johnson County in the 2d District as damaging to Tauke. Again, the plan was defeated, 24-26.

Had the legislators voted "no" a third time, redistricting would have fallen into their hands. But by this time, public grumblings were being heard about legisla-

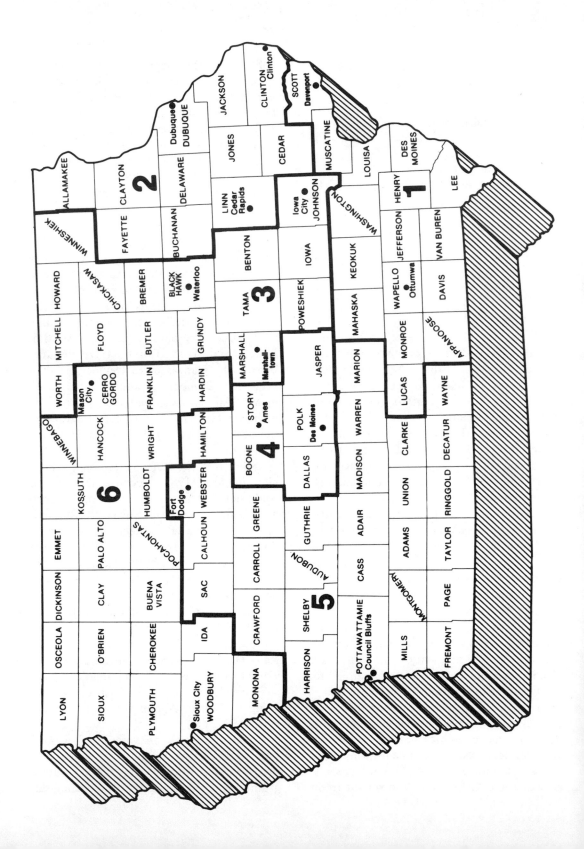

tors' playing politics with the process. In August, when the bureau issued its third plan, it was approved by a 39-10 vote in the Senate and by 92-5 in the state House— despite the protests of GOP representative Cooper Evans over the transfer of Johnson County into his 3d District. (Evans survived, but upon his retirement in 1986, Democrat Dave Nagle won the contest to succeed him.)

While the members of the House delegation—one of whom will lose his seat in the post-1990 remap—might prefer more personal control over the process, neither party has shown any sentiment to change the nonpartisan redistricting law.

Over the decade the Democrats have captured firm control of both houses of the Legislature (30-20 in the Senate; 61-39 in the House), but they recognize that GOP governor Terry E. Branstad—if he is reelected in 1990—would veto any partisan plan Democrats could produce. Because the Legislature has a diminished role in the mapmaking process, Democratic legislators are also less likely to be targets of the national GOP's efforts to win legislative majorities in 1990.

For Iowa Republicans, whose chances of regaining a majority in either house next year are a long shot, the nonpartisan linedrawing process gives them some cover against Democratic machinations. "We are distrustful of what a Democratic majority would try to do," said Iowa Republican party chairman Richard Schwarm.

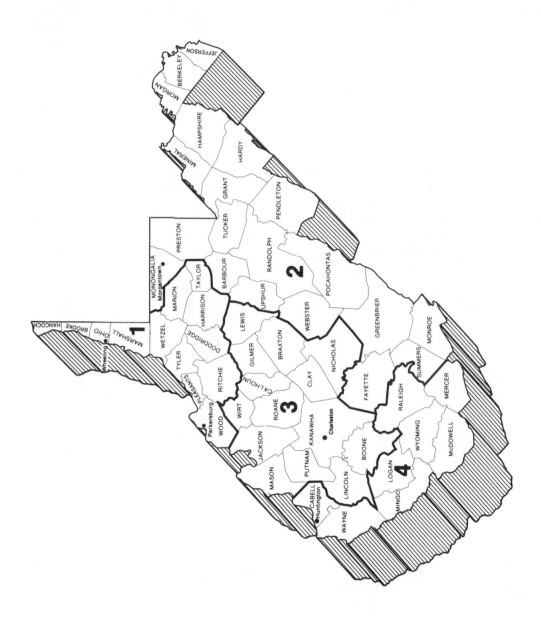

West Virginia

Population and growth

1980 population	1,949,644
1989 population estimate	1,857,000
(34th in the nation)	
Percent change 1980-1989	-5%

U.S. Congress

Senate 2 D
House 4 D

State legislature

Senate 30 D, 4 R
House 80 D, 20 R
Governor Gaston Caperton, D

Troubled by the downward spiral of its coal and steel industries, West Virginia was one of only two states—Iowa was the other—that lost population between 1980 and 1989, according to Census Bureau estimates. This 5 percent decline is likely to cost the state one of its four House seats after 1990.

Adjusting for that loss could provoke a Democratic family feud. Democrats hold all elements of the redistricting process, with a 30-4 edge in the state Senate (half of the seats are up in 1990), an 80-20 state House majority, and the governorship (Gov. Gaston Caperton is not up until 1992). But all four members of the U.S. House delegation—Nick J. Rahall II, Alan B. Mollohan, Harley O. Staggers, Jr., and Bob Wise—are also Democrats. Thus, the Democratic mapmakers will have to ax one of their own.

Each member has some advantage he can try to use as a trump card. Rahall is the senior member and is chairman of the Interior Subcommittee on Mining. Wise, whose district includes the state capital of Charleston, is seen as the delegation's rising star. Mollohan's position on House Appropriations has enabled him to obtain federal dollars for his northern panhandle district. Staggers's eastern district, which reaches into the Washington, D.C., exurbs, is showing signs of growth. In addition, Mollohan and Staggers have family ties to call on: their fathers—Robert Mollohan and Harley O. Staggers, Sr.—were House members.

There has been some speculation about who might be paired in 1992, but no one has a clear idea of how redistricting will unfold. West Virginia University professor David Bingham said he does not expect the state legislators to do anything about redistricting in advance of the release of the 1990 census data. "They don't want to make enemies too soon," he said.

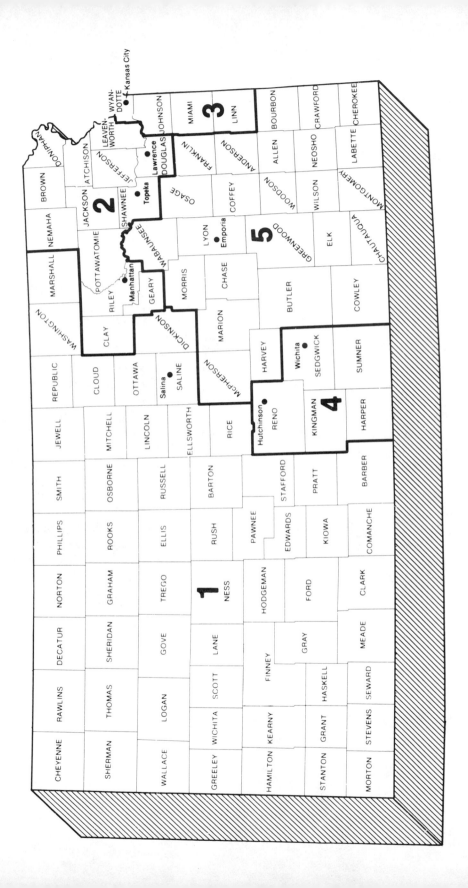

Kansas

Population and growth

1980 population	2,363,679
1989 population estimate	2,513,000
(32d in the nation)	
Percent change 1980-1989	+6%

U.S. Congress

Senate	2 R
House	2 D, 3 R

State legislature

Senate	18 D, 22 R
House	57 D, 68 R
Governor	Mike Hayden, R

The long-term shrinkage of its farm-based population and a decline in the energy-resource industries in southern parts of the state have placed Kansas at risk of losing a congressional seat after 1990. It would be Kansas's first seat loss since the 1960s; with four districts for the 1990s, Kansas would have exactly half its peak total of eight, which it held from 1891-1931.

How difficult this downward adjustment will be has already been the subject of much discussion, because of a series of career decisions by members of the Kansas congressional delegation. In early 1989 there was speculation that two-term Republican senator Nancy Landon Kassebaum would not seek reelection in 1990. Had that happened, redistricting might have been relatively painless: veteran House members such as Democrat Dan Glickman and Republicans Pat Roberts and Jan Meyers were viewed as likely Senate candidates.

But Kassebaum announced that she would run for a third Senate term, and none of the House members will challenge her. The redistricting picture was further complicated when Democratic representative

Jim Slattery, expected to challenge Republican governor Mike Hayden, opted to run for reelection instead.

However, a possible solution to the state's redistricting woes suddenly presented itself with 5th District Republican representative Bob Whittaker's surprise decision that he would not seek reelection in 1990. The 5th District, which will therefore have a freshman member serving at the time of redistricting, may be a logical target for elimination. Moreover, with its flagging farm, coal, and oil sectors, the 5th lost some residents between 1980 and 1986.

That the 5th will be dismembered if Kansas loses a seat has become conventional wisdom in the state. Several high-profile members of both parties demurred from the contest to succeed Whittaker because of the expectation that it would be a one-term job; several of the primary contenders for the seat felt compelled to state publicly that they would run for reelection in 1992, regardless of how the map is redrawn.

Whittaker's step out of the way takes some pressure off other members of the delegation. Only Meyers appeared secure: her 3d District, which includes the affluent Johnson County suburbs of Kansas City, Missouri, grew by more than 10 percent in the early 1980s. Roberts's 1st District, an expanse of wheat fields and rangeland already sprawling across fifty-eight counties, has had minimal population growth. And while Slattery's 2d (Topeka) and Glickman's 4th (Wichita) have done somewhat better, both members are Democrats facing a redistricting process that is likely to be controlled by Republicans.

Republicans are assured of holding at least one leg of the redistricting tripod: they have a 22-18 majority in the state Senate, which has no 1990 elections. The Democrats, even after a seven-seat gain in 1988, have to win six more state House seats in

1990 to overcome their 68-57 deficit.

However, state Democrats are touting their chances to unseat Hayden. The first-term governor's popularity plummeted in 1988 when he failed to pursue legislation to rebate a state tax windfall (a result of the 1986 federal tax code revision) to Kansas residents. Hayden's aggressive promotion of a tax-relief measure in 1989 stabilized his position, but he was again blistered in early 1990 by another tax revolt, this one resulting from soaring property assessments. Hayden's troubles have spurred a comeback attempt by his predecessor, Democrat John Carlin, who is running in the August 7 Democratic primary.

6

States Gaining Seats

Texas

Population and growth

1980 population	14,229,191
1989 population estimate (3d in the nation)	16,991,000
Percent change 1980-1989	+19%

U.S. Congress

Senate	1 D, 1 R
House	19 D, 8 R

State legislature

Senate	23 D, 8 R
House	90 D, 60 R
Governor	William P. Clements, Jr., R

Although its previously explosive growth was tempered by an economic slump in the second half of the 1980s, Texas is still projected to gain three House seats after the 1990 census, the same number it added after the last enumeration. The Census Bureau estimated that between 1980 and 1989 Texas's population increased by more than 19 percent.

Some of the individual House districts have grown at an even greater pace. According to Census Bureau estimates covering 1980 to 1986, Texas's 26th District, between Fort Worth and Dallas, had a 42 percent population increase, the fastest growth rate in the country; the Austin-based 10th District ranked third, with a 33 percent increase.

Early in the 1980s the state GOP announced a plan to win control of at least one house of the Legislature in time for the post-1990 redistricting. But in spite of continued gains, particularly in the House, Republicans remain far short of this goal, with just one election left before the remap. The Democrats' apparently firm hold on the Legislature has raised the stakes in the 1990 election to succeed retiring Republican governor William P. Clements, Jr.

When the Republicans announced their ambitious legislative goal, they were understandably met with disbelief: the Democrats held majorities of 26-5 in the Senate and 114-36 in the House after the 1982 elections.

The GOP made noticeable headway in 1984. Aided by the Reagan landslide, the party gained sixteen seats in the House. In more recent elections, however, that momentum has been slowed. Even after a two-seat net GOP gain in the Senate in 1988, the Democratic majority remains a sturdy 23-8 (half the seats are up in 1990). And despite a major Republican push in 1988—which included a $750,000 investment by GOP-oriented political action committees in

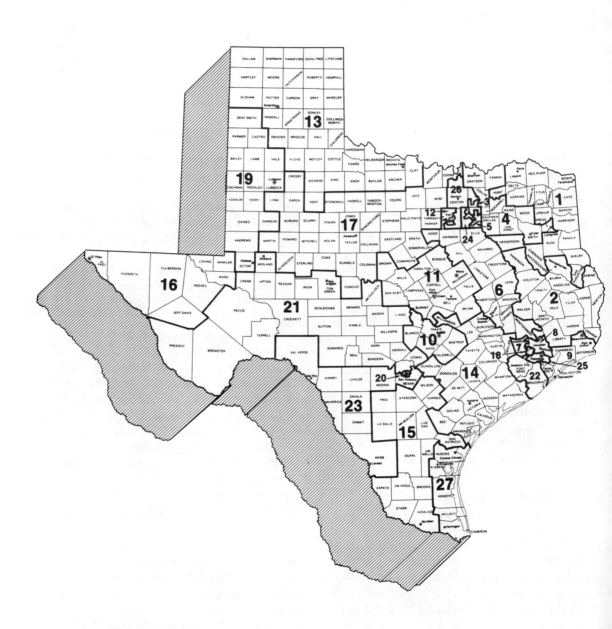

the final five weeks of the campaign—the Republicans gained a net of just two House seats.

In 1989 Republicans won close special elections in two formerly Democratic House districts in Houston. Also, one Democratic House member switched to the GOP, closing the Democratic margin to 90-60. Texas GOP chairman Fred Meyer notes that in thirty-two Democratic-held House districts, the party registration is more favorable to Republicans than in those Houston special-election districts. But Democratic officials think their legislators will be ready for Republican challengers. "1984 woke a whole lot of our legislators up," said Texas Democratic executive director Ed Martin.

Unlike in 1984 and 1988, Martin said, Democratic legislative candidates next year will not be saddled with a presidential standard-bearer widely viewed in conservative-minded Texas as a soft-on-defense, soft-on-crime northern liberal. "The national tickets have offered us terrible symbolism," he said. Presidential candidate Michael S. Dukakis carried only 43 percent of the state's 1988 vote, even with Sen. Lloyd Bentsen of Texas as his running mate.

However, even the most rose-colored Democratic outlook for 1990 does not foresee the ten-seat rebound needed to restore the party to a veto-proof House majority in time for redistricting. Much of the GOP's House progress has stemmed from Republicans' replacing traditional southern Democrats (usually after retirements) in districts that had otherwise shown strong conservative Republican tendencies. Democrats are unlikely to roll back these gains any time soon.

While the slower-growing Senate Republican caucus remains somewhat in the shadows, the House Republicans have gained unprecedented influence. A coalition of Republicans and conservative Democrats has played a prominent role on some major

legislative issues since the mid-1980s. Democratic House Speaker Gib Lewis, a conservative from Fort Worth, has pursued an unusual policy of outreach, including appointing nine Republicans as committee chairmen. "He has the delusion that he can still run the House in this nonpartisan fashion," said Dave Denison, editor of the *Texas Observer,* which has a generally liberal orientation.

This bipartisan demeanor could carry over into the redistricting process. There is precedent for this sort of neutrality in Texas redistricting. Some Democrats even say former Democratic Speaker Billy Clayton went overboard during the last congressional redistricting, allying himself with Governor Clements and leading a group of conservative Democrats in support of a plan that appeared highly favorable to Republicans. However, a federal district court overturned that plan, ruling under the Voting Rights Act that the map unnecessarily divided Hispanic concentrations in south Texas among several districts. Revisions in 1982 and 1983 were somewhat more favorable to the Democrats.

Lewis's press secretary, Tim Conger, struck a conciliatory note in talking about redistricting. "I don't anticipate it taking an overly partisan tone," he said. But Conger said Lewis's partisan instincts could be reawakened if Republicans target entrenched House Democrats (including Lewis, who remembers a 1986 challenge). "The Speaker has always been fair," Conger said. "But you never know what kind of mental transition you will experience when you've gone through a bloody campaign."

Said Democratic representative Tom Uher, Lewis's appointee as chairman of the Reapportionment Committee: "As we've become more of a two-party state, there will be less and less cooperation. There are more and more challengers. As [the Republicans] go after those seats, there will be increasing friction." But he added that even the most hard-line Democratic partisans will be constrained by the need to accommodate the real Republican growth, in registration and office-holding, in many areas of Texas.

Republican U.S. representative Dick Armey serves the blossoming 26th District; of the nine other districts with growth rates of 20 percent or more through 1986, Republicans hold six. "I don't think you can exempt partisanship . . . ," Uher said, "but you have to start looking at what is reality." Martin concurred, saying it may be hard to "screw them out of seats. . . . Demography may be shifting a bit the other way."

Uher also said the interests of House members of both parties will be duly noted in the next remap. "I don't think we should throw everybody out and start from scratch. . . . We need experienced people. . . . My door will be open to them."

Whatever the Legislature's craftwork, it may be rendered moot. In both the 1970s and the 1980s, Texas's congressional redistricting was remanded to the courtroom, as the cross-cutting ambitions of incumbents, party activists, urban blacks, and south Texas Hispanics came into conflict. Those involved in the 1990s process say it is likely to happen again. "Place one census tract into a certain alignment and you may have [affected] the goals or aspirations of a certain group," said Uher. "I expect any plans to be challenged in court."

Florida

Population and growth

1980 population	9,746,324
1989 population estimate	12,671,000
(4th in the nation)	
Percent change 1980-1989	+30%

U.S. Congress

Senate 1 D, 1 R
House 8 D, 11 R

State legislature

Senate 23 D, 17 R
House 72 D, 48 R
Governor Bob Martinez, R

Brimming with new residents from the Frost Belt and the tropics, Florida continues to climb in the ranks of America's megastates. With its population estimated at 12.7 million in 1989, Florida appears certain to gain three, and quite possibly four, House seats. These gains will give Florida as many as twenty-three House seats—this in a state that had just eight when John F. Kennedy was elected president in 1960.

Florida's hopes of obtaining that fourth additional seat may depend on whether all the illegal aliens who have arrived in the state from Central and South America, Cuba, and Haiti since the 1980 census are counted. Florida officials have joined a coalition with those from similarly affected states to block efforts by states with few immigrants to exclude illegal aliens from the 1990 count.

Whatever the gain turns out to be, it will be no easy matter deciding where to put the new districts. Few areas have been untouched by growth: from 1980 to 1986 the population increase in all but four of the nineteen House districts was estimated in double-digit percentages.

The political demographics of Florida's boom have national and state GOP officials rubbing their hands in expectation of House gains. The GOP has made huge voter-registration advances during the 1980s, thanks to an influx of many midwestern Republicans, whom some state pols refer to as "Taft people" (after longtime Ohio GOP senator Robert A. Taft), and thanks to party switching by traditional southern Democrats among the native population. From 1980 to 1988 the GOP reduced the Democratic registration advantage from 3.9 million-1.4 million to 3.3 million-2.4 million.

The Republican upswing has also been obvious at the polls. Florida's U.S. House delegation, which was 13-6 Democratic after the 1982 elections, now has an 11-8 GOP edge. Republicans have picked up four seats just since the 1988 elections. In those contests, Republicans Craig T. James and Cliff Stearns scored upsets in Democratic-held districts. In February 1989 Democratic representative Bill Grant switched parties. In August Republican Ileana Ros-Lehtinen became the first Cuban-American in Congress, winning a special election to succeed the late Democratic representative Claude Pepper.

In looking forward to more gains in the 1990s, Republican strategists note that Florida's most rapidly developing areas—those most likely to share in the added House seats—have been trending Republican in recent years. Of the eight fastest-growing House districts (all of which had estimated population growth of 24 percent or more through 1986), six—the 4th, 5th, 6th, 9th, 12th, and 13th—are represented by Republicans. The 11th, although held by Democrat Bill Nelson, a 1990 gubernatorial candidate, gave 70 percent of its presidential vote to George Bush in 1988. The 14th (Broward and Palm Beach counties) is the other district held by a Democrat, freshman Harry A. Johnston.

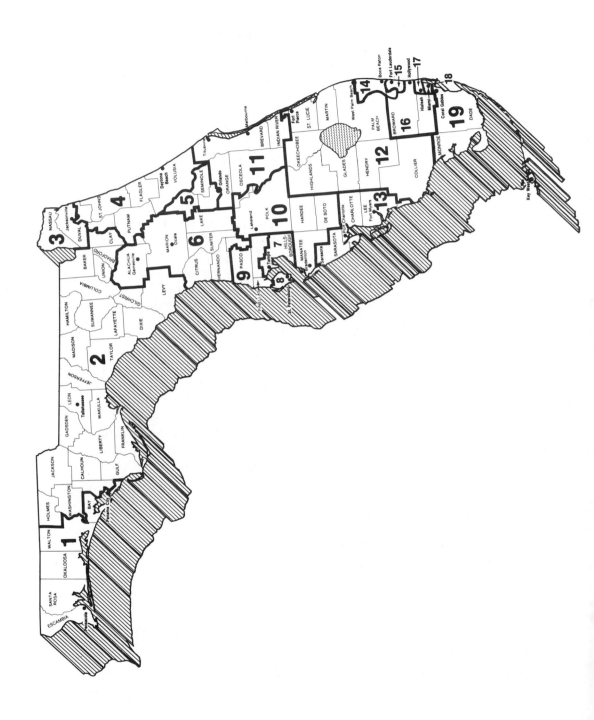

Republicans also enter the 1990 state-level elections—the last before redistricting—in their strongest position this century. With Bob Martinez, Republicans hold the governorship for just the second time since Reconstruction. In the Senate a 32-8 Democratic majority after the 1982 elections has shrunk to 23-17, and GOP strategists are touting their chances for a takeover in 1990. A twelve-seat gain in the House since 1982 still leaves the GOP down 48-72, but that is enough to deny Democrats the two-thirds majority they would need to pass a redistricting plan over Martinez's veto.

The cloud in this sunny Republican scenario is Martinez's uncertain reelection outlook. Elected in 1986, Martinez, a former Tampa mayor, was damaged politically by his support of a services tax increase during his first year in office. By mid-1989 Martinez's strong stands against drug trafficking and for capital punishment seemed to give him a boost with the electorate just in time for his 1990 campaign. But then he again put himself at risk.

Immediately after the Supreme Court's *Webster v. Reproductive Health Services* decision in July 1989, Martinez emerged as a leading anti-abortion spokesman, appearing on national TV advocating an outright ban on abortion except in cases of rape, incest, or danger to the woman. He called for a special session of the Legislature in October to consider restricting abortions. But public opinion polls soon indicated that Martinez had raced out in front of a more moderate voter consensus.

Democrats and pro-abortion rights Republicans besieged Martinez, but he also was beseeched by conservative GOP legislators: while they generally agreed with him on abortion, they feared the issue could undercut their efforts to capture the swing districts they need for a Senate majority. "We tried to counsel the governor, 'Stay out of it for a while,' " said Senate Minority Leader William G. "Doc" Myers, an abortion foe who opposed the special session. "He put legislators on the spot. . . . It could stop our drive to take over" the Senate.

Still, Martinez pressed ahead. The October special session ended swiftly and predictably. Unable to overcome the opposition of the Democratic majority and the reluctance of many Republicans, Martinez saw his proposals to restrict abortion crushed in committees; none reached the floor.

Even if Martinez recovers to run strongly for reelection, Democrats are still in front to keep a majority in the Senate. In 1988 Democrats limited the GOP to a two-seat Senate gain, even as Bush was rolling up 61 percent of Florida's presidential vote.

Some analysts think Republicans may not need a Senate majority to influence redistricting. A group of Republicans and conservative Democrats has held sway in that body since 1986; even a decade ago, a conservative coalition, including a smaller Republican caucus, was influential in a congressional remap that resulted in Republican wins in two of the four new seats.

But the new, more aggressive profile of Florida's GOP may awaken partisan instincts among more Democrats, making compromise and concessions harder to reach in the next round of redistricting.

"The process will inevitably be much more partisan than ten years ago," said Democrat Peter Rudy Wallace, chairman of the House Reapportionment Committee. "Every legislative decision now turns on conditions of partisanship that weren't there before."

But it will be impossible to deprive Florida's surging GOP of a share of the redistricting booty. "We want to elect Democrats to Congress, and we would love to recapture the Democratic majority" in the U.S. House delegation, said Wallace. "But . . . there are many more Republicans than in the past."

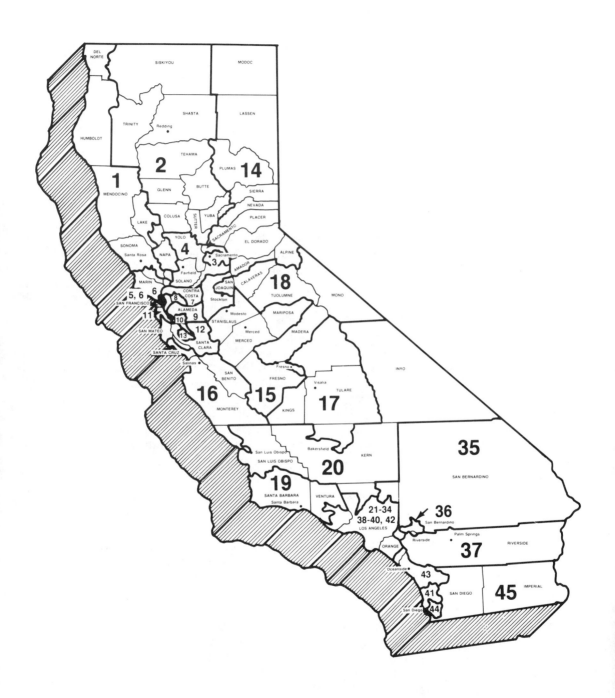

California

Population and growth

1980 population	23,667,902
1989 population estimate	29,063,000
(1st in the nation)	
Percent change 1980-1989	+23%

U.S. Congress

Senate 1 D, 1 R
House 27 D, 18 R

State legislature

Senate 24 D, 13 R, 1 Ind., 2 Vacancies
House 46 D, 33 R, 1 Vacancy
Governor George Deukmejian, R

The land of congressional opportunity and font of redistricting controversy, California will be the most-watched state when House district lines are redrawn after 1990.

The domestic migration to California, combined with a huge influx of immigrants (legal and illegal) from Mexico, Central and South America, and Asia, has pushed the population of America's nation-state from 23.7 million in 1980 to more than 29 million in 1989. Reapportionment experts project that this increase will earn California a bounty of at least six new House seats. A seven-seat gain is more than an outside possibility, especially if the minority-group residents are fully counted.

Either way, California, which already has more than a tenth of all House members, appears certain to become the first state to break the fifty-seat barrier, smashing the record of forty-five it shares with New York, which elected that many members from 1932 through 1950.

Yet it is the method of redistricting, rather than the numbers involved, that will draw the attention of politicos from around the country. The state's Democrats and Republicans are preparing to rejoin the battle that has raged over redistricting since January 1982.

In 1982 a House district map highly favorable to the Democrats was drawn by Democratic representative Phillip Burton, rushed through the Democratic-controlled Legislature, and signed by Democratic governor Edmund G. Brown, Jr. Given the loud, angry, and persistent GOP complaints about the plan, it is surprising that "Burtonizing" has not supplanted the nineteenth-century term "gerrymandering" to describe partisan redistricting.

Even as they fought a six-year court battle to reverse Burton's plan, California Republicans pursued an effort to prevent a repeat in the 1990s by capturing the Legislature. But apparently they have failed: with just the 1990 contests left, Democrats maintain majorities of 24-13-1 (with two vacancies) in the Senate, where half the seats are up in 1990, and 46-33 (with one vacancy) in the Assembly.

Republicans have thus turned their attention to keeping the governor's veto power in GOP hands. Republican governor George Deukmejian is retiring after two terms, but his party recruited U.S. senator Pete Wilson to run in 1990. But even Wilson's seemingly advantageous position provides insufficient assurance for state Republicans; he will have to engage in a big-spending brawl with the winner of the June 1990 Democratic gubernatorial primary between former San Francisco mayor Dianne Feinstein and state attorney general John Van de Kamp.

So as insurance against losing the governorship, several state Republicans developed ballot initiative proposals in 1989 that would change, or even eliminate, the Legislature's role in redistricting. Two of these proposals—one that would take the redistricting process out of the Legislature and turn it over to an independent commission, and the other that would require a "super majority" in the Legislature to pass a redistricting plan—received enough petition signatures to qualify for the June primary ballot. Given the immense size of California's congressional delegation and the state's reputation as a national trendsetter, the outcome of this debate over remap methodology could have a big impact on other states.

California's partisan redistricting dispute began in 1981, during deliberations over how to rework the U.S. House district map to include two new seats. Although the Legislature, then as now, had secure Democratic majorities, the competing demands and ambitions of its members led to a redistricting stalemate. In stepped Burton, a redistricting expert who had worked on the remaps of the 1960s and the 1970s as a legislator and then as a U.S. House member. Using his extensive knowledge of California demographics and working mainly with a hand-held calculator, Burton crafted a forty-five district plan that friends and foes alike described as a masterwork of partisan redistricting. Burton described it as "my contribution to modern art."

The new map abounded with gyrating lines, narrow fingers, and other contrivances, creating districts designed to connect (or avoid) partisan concentrations. Unlike redistricting craftsmen in most states that gained seats, Burton did not merely provide the majority party with advantages in the newly gained districts; he completely redrew the map, especially in fast-growing Southern California, dismembering three Republican-held districts and providing new opportunities for Democrats of the Los Angeles-based political organization associated with Democratic representative Henry A. Waxman and state representative Howard L. Berman (elected to Congress in 1982). Without even viewing the map, both houses of the Legislature approved it just before adjourning in September 1981.

Republicans cried foul, pointing out

that the Democratic plan had eliminated Republican seats even though the strongest growth had been in the suburban, Republican-oriented areas of Los Angeles and Orange counties. The GOP then embarked on an ill-fated effort to revoke Burton's plan. It had some initial success, persuading voters to pass a June 1982 initiative requiring the Legislature to redraw the map after the 1982 elections. However, the revised plan made only minor changes that did not alter the Democrats' edge; this map was passed in a special session and signed into law by retiring governor Brown just before Republican Deukmejian took office in January 1983. Another GOP initiative drive was staged that year, but the state Supreme Court, which then had a Democratic majority, ruled it off the ballot.

The rest of the Republican effort took place mainly in the courtroom. Then-U.S. representative Robert E. Badham sued the state, claiming that Burton's plan was a blatant gerrymander that violated Republican voters' rights to representation. By the time the case reached the U.S. Supreme Court, the plaintiffs in *Eu v. San Francisco County Democratic Central Committee* had renewed hope: the Court had ruled in a 1986 Indiana case, *Davis v. Bandemer,* that partisan criteria could be considered in gerrymandering cases. In 1982 a 22-21 Democratic majority in California's U.S. House delegation widened to 28-17 under Burton's map; only one seat switched to the Republicans in ensuing elections, in which most of the victorious House candidates (of both parties) won with at least 60 percent. However, the Supreme Court upheld the lower court decision against the Republicans without issuing an opinion. Its ruling, which completed the long redistricting process for the decade, was handed down in January 1989—nearly six years after Burton had died of a heart attack.

During this period, California Republicans aimed to guarantee themselves a voice in the 1990s process by waging aggressive, targeted campaigns for legislative seats. But the Democratic party, bolstered by the fund-raising abilities of its legislative leadership (especially Assembly Speaker Willie L. Brown, Jr.), parried every GOP thrust. In 1988, despite a Republican presidential victory in California, Democrats held even in the Senate and gained two seats in the Assembly. After nearly a decade of striving, the Republicans have just two more Assembly seats—and two fewer Senate seats—than they did after the 1980 elections.

The Republican failure to gain ground in 1988 legislative races fueled the movement within the GOP to come up with an initiative plan that either would take redrawing the lines out of the Legislature's hands and assign it to an independent commission or would at least provide some guarantee of a Republican role in redistricting. In mid-1989 more than a half-dozen proposals were being circulated. But by the end of the year, the two proposals that had attracted the most support from political and public-interest activists had the field to themselves.

The measure that would maintain the Legislature's primary role was proposed by Marin County businessman Gary J. Flynn. The initiative would require that any redistricting proposal pass the Legislature by a two-thirds majority, thus guaranteeing a say for the Republicans, who hold well over a third of the seats in each house.

The Flynn proposal, which has the support of the Republican National Committee as well as that of Republican legislators who want to preserve their role in the process, also attempts to place redistricting within the rubric of government "ethics." Along with establishing "fair" criteria for district boundaries and allowing for referendums on redistricting plans, the initiative would also create an Ethics Committee to enforce standards of conduct in the Legislature.

The other initiative proposal on the June 1990 ballot was drawn up by San Mateo County Supervisor Tom Huening. It would create a twelve-member "Independent Citizens Redistricting Commission" to be appointed by a panel of retired state appellate judges. This commission would be empowered to select from redistricting plans submitted by any number of political entities, activist groups, and individual citizens. The Heuning proposal attracted support from several "good government" groups, including the League of Women Voters.

Republican officials express confidence about the prospects of the passage of one of these measures (if both receive a majority, the one with the higher vote total would become law). U.S. representative Bill Thomas, a Republican activist on redistricting, cited what he described as a growing public concern about government ethics. He said Republicans will use the argument that "these people [the legislators] draw their own lines, folks. . . . There is a degree of self-dealing that goes on."

But even as they work to create a voting constituency behind the initiative concept, the Republicans will have a chore winning the unbridled enthusiasm of some of their own party's elected officials for a sweeping adjustment of the district map. Early in the decade, the anti-Burton forces received only tacit support from some members of the Republican House delegation. They were not so unhappy with Burton's map, because in drawing so many districts to be winnable by Democrats, Burton made the remaining districts safe havens for Republicans.

Thomas, a member of a House Republican Conference working group and of a California GOP task force on redistricting, said one of the goals of the GOP redistricting activists is to prevent Republicans from being co-opted by such perks. "Our broader concern as a party is that the only thing worse than a partisan gerrymander is a bipartisan gerrymander," he said.

Democrats are not lying low in the face of the Republican efforts to change the system. In August 1989 Speaker Brown turned his fifty-dollar-per-person end-of-session party, which traditionally has gone to benefit legislative candidates, into a fundraiser for the Committee for Fair Reapportionment, which he chairs. The money "will be used to oppose reapportionment initiatives that are bad for California," said Susan Jetton, Brown's press secretary at that time. "So far, he hasn't seen any good reapportionment initiatives."

Even if redistricting is handled through the legislative process, duplicating Burton's feat will not be easy. Much of the state's growth has been in affluent, Republican-leaning areas of Southern California, particularly in the suburbs and exurbs of Los Angeles and San Diego, and in the booming Riverside-San Bernardino area. According to Census Bureau estimates, all forty-five California districts gained population through 1986, and thirty-three were up by 10 percent or more. But of the seven districts with growth rates of more than 20 percent, Republicans hold five—the 37th, 35th, 14th, 20th, 43d—while just the 36th and 18th are in Democratic hands. "It is hard to imagine any Republicans' being jeopardized," said GOP representative Thomas.

Political observers say there is another factor portending a redistricting process somewhat less politically charged than last time: while there are many aggressively partisan and talented Democrats in California—including Tony Coelho, former U.S. House majority whip; Vic Fazio, current House Democratic Caucus vice chairman; and Michael Berman, Democratic consultant and brother of U.S. representative Howard Berman—insiders have not singled out any of them as the obvious successor to Burton, who viewed redistricting as an intellectual as well as a political pursuit. "Phillip was one of a kind. . . . No one knew reapportionment like him," said his brother, state representative John Burton, a former member of Congress. "He could go through people's districts in other states and could tell what the growth patterns would be."

The difficulty of evading the Republicans' apparent demographic gains, as well as concerns about a possible antigerrymander backlash among voters, has spurred some Democrats to express interest in a bipartisan approach to the next redistricting. But Thomas said the suggestions he has heard would place only the state's new House seats on the table, while carefully protecting the gains Democrats crafted for themselves in 1982. Thomas, who thinks his party was rolled last time and wants the whole map revised, strongly favors the initiative route over what he sees as a Democratic-oriented compromise. "When you've got nothing to lose," he said, "why not roll the dice?"

Arizona

Population and growth

1980 population	2,718,215
1989 population estimate	3,556,000
(24th in the nation)	
Percent change 1980-1989	+31%

U.S. Congress

Senate	1 D,	1 R
House	1 D,	4 R

State legislature

Senate	13 D,	17 R
House	26 D,	34 R
Governor	Rose Mofford, D	

With a population that increased by nearly 31 percent from 1980 to 1989, Arizona is poised to gain a House seat for the third straight decade, and it may gain two.

Republican strategists see the population shift from northern industrial states to conservative Sun Belt states such as Arizona as a guarantee of House gains in the 1990s. Arizona was one of fifteen states to give 60 percent or more of its presidential vote to Republican George Bush in 1988. The same year, Republicans—a minor factor in state politics until the rise of Barry Goldwater in the late 1950s—finally overcame conservative Democratic traditions by gaining a plurality in voter registration.

At the local level, the state's greatest population growth has been in U.S. House districts represented by Republicans. The 1st, a Phoenix-area district held by Republican John J. Rhodes III, grew by an estimated 33 percent from 1980 to 1986. The Republican 4th (represented by Jon Kyl) and 3d (Bob Stump) grew by more than 20 percent, with Jim Kolbe's 5th hitting double digits at 11 percent. The Tucson-based 2d, held by veteran Democrat Morris K. Udall, had a more modest population increase of about 7 percent.

But state-level political realities do not portend a Republican-dominated redistricting process. Democratic governor Rose Mofford, who replaced impeached Republican governor Evan Mecham in 1988, decided not to run for the office in 1990; but as the campaign got under way, former Phoenix mayor Terry Goddard appeared to have a strong chance to keep the governorship in Democratic hands. In the Legislature, once-commanding Republican majorities were narrowed to 17-13 in the Senate and 34-26 in the House in 1988, when Democrats gained two seats in each.

That the Republican trend at the federal level has seemingly reversed in state politics can be traced mainly to the turmoil surrounding Mecham. A hard-right activist and six-time loser for statewide office, Mecham turned Arizona politics upside down in 1986, defeating the GOP establishment's choice for governor in a primary, then winning the office with a 40 percent plurality in a three-way race. But his backers' efforts to gain control of the state GOP apparatus created intraparty schisms that turned into canyons after a series of controversial actions and statements by Mecham during his first year in office.

When accusations of financial irregularities in Mecham's 1986 campaign came to light, many members of his own party felt no loyalty to him. In April 1988 he was convicted and evicted by the Republican-controlled Senate, even though Democrat Mofford, then the secretary of state, was next in line to succeed him.

Angry Mecham backers retaliated by running against anti-Mecham Republican legislators in several 1988 primaries, and they scored a few knockouts. These provided some of the opportunities that led to Democratic gains. For example, a Mecham Republican who ousted House Speaker Joe Lane in the primary lost in turn to a

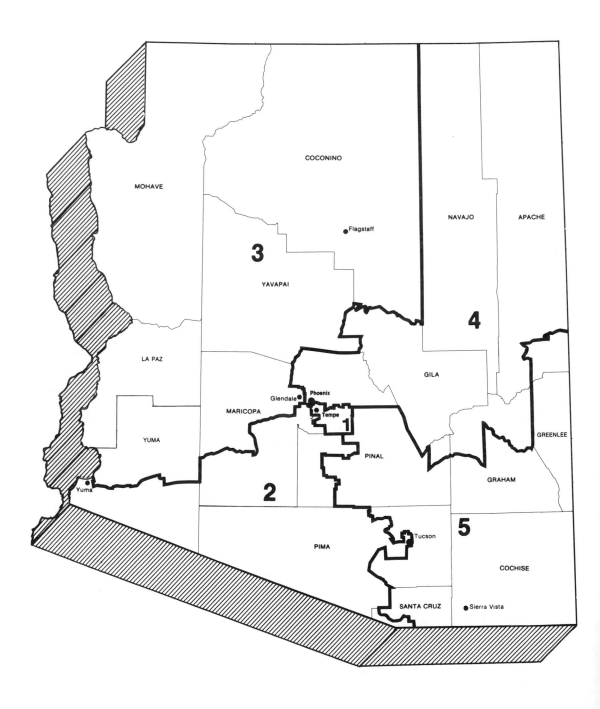

MOHAVE

COCONINO

NAVAJO   APACHE

• Flagstaff

3

YAVAPAI

4

LA PAZ

GILA

GREENLEE

Glendale •   • Phoenix

MARICOPA   • Tempe

1

YUMA

PINAL

GRAHAM

• Yuma

2

5

• Tucson

PIMA

COCHISE

SANTA CRUZ   • Sierra Vista

Democrat in the general election.

Despite the Democratic gains in 1988, Republicans point out that they limited their losses and survived the tumultuous year with their legislative majorities intact. "[The Democrats'] best shot at major inroads similar to Watergate came in 1988," said Rep. Chris Herstam, a "mainstream" Republican. "The voters didn't hold Mecham against us as a party."

But there is still worry among mainstream Republicans that Mecham loyalists will cause trouble in 1990 legislative primaries. "I would not be surprised if there is a group of those people who will run in predominantly Republican areas against establishment Republicans," said Senate Majority Leader John T. Mawhinney.

Mecham has announced plans to run in the 1990 Republican gubernatorial primary. Mawhinney expressed chagrin at even the possibility of his renomination. "Those of us who impeached him could not find it in our hearts to support him," he said. "It would be a significant setback for the Arizona Republican Party."

The turbulent political atmosphere in Arizona has left legislators with little time to dwell on the upcoming congressional redistricting. "People are more interested in saving their necks in the next election than about redistricting," said Herstam.

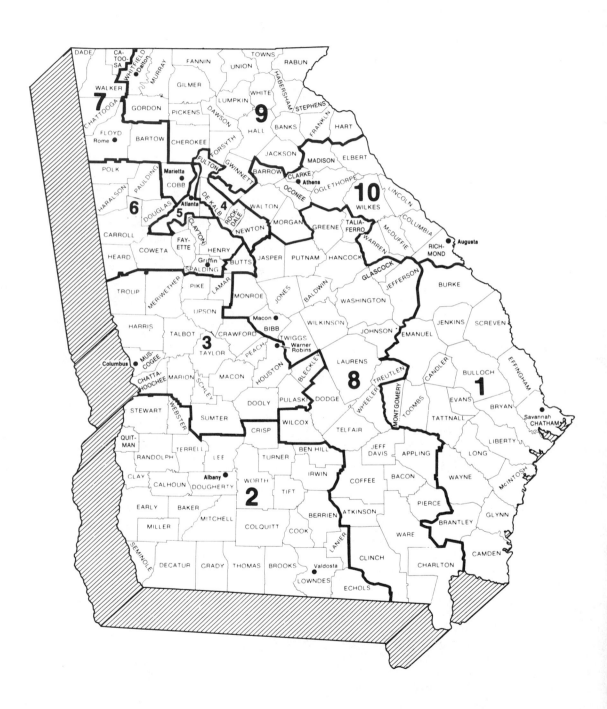

Georgia

Population and growth

1980 population	5,463,105
1989 population estimate	6,438,000
(11th in the nation)	
Percent change 1980-1989	+18%

U.S. Congress

Senate 2 D
House 9 D, 1 R

State legislature

Senate 45 D, 11 R
House 144 D, 36 R
Governor Joe Frank Harris, D

With Atlanta's business boom spurring an estimated state population increase of about 18 percent through 1989, Georgia seems certain to gain a House seat, and possibly a second, after the next census. Any new seats would almost certainly be in the Atlanta metropolitan area.

Although Atlanta's inner-city 5th District grew only slightly during the 1980s, the suburban districts exploded. Population in the inner-suburban 4th District grew by 13 percent from 1980 to 1986. Even this growth rate was dwarfed by that in surrounding districts, which take in much rural territory but reach into Atlanta's outer suburbs. The 9th and 10th, which share rapidly developing Gwinnett County, have both experienced growth of 20 percent or more during the decade. However, this bounty has not been shared by the less affluent, farm-oriented areas of southern Georgia: the southwestern 2d District, for example, had grown by only 3 percent through 1986.

Therefore, major changes will have to be made to Georgia's congressional district map. Although the GOP has a shot—albeit a long one—at the governorship, which Democrat Joe Frank Harris is leaving after two terms, the Democrats have a strong grip on the redistricting pen in the Legislature, which still has a Southern Democratic color. Republicans are a distinct minority, trailing 45-11 in the Senate (where all seats are up in 1990), and 144-36 in the House (even after a seven-seat gain in 1988).

Even with this dominance, it will be difficult for Democrats to avoid basing a new district in heavily Republican Gwinnett County, which gave George Bush 75 percent of its 1988 presidential vote. Efforts to insulate conservative, rural-oriented Democratic incumbents by divesting them of other suburban territory also may benefit the GOP.

However, it is not far-fetched to expect that Democrats may use their redistricting strength to make trouble for the Georgia delegation's sole Republican: Newt Gingrich, the House minority whip and Democrat antagonist extraordinaire. Gingrich has what could kindly be described as an unfriendly relationship with state House Speaker Thomas B. Murphy, whose Haralson County base is in Gingrich's 6th District.

An old-fashioned legislative clout-wielder and potentially the most powerful player in the next redistricting, Murphy has portrayed Gingrich's efforts to build the local Republican party as an invasion of his turf. And Murphy accused Gingrich of orchestrating a 1988 challenge to him by a conservative Republican. At the state GOP's May 1989 convention, Gingrich rejected the portrayal of Murphy and his courthouse Democrat allies as "good old boys," describing them instead as "pleasant people who behind the scenes are thugs."

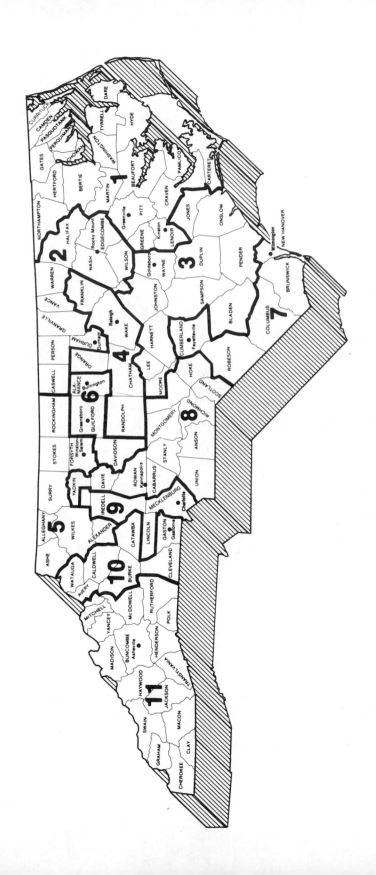

7

Borderline States

North Carolina

Population and growth

1980 population	5,881,766
1989 population estimate	6,571,000
(10th in the nation)	
Percent change 1980-1989	+12%

U.S. Congress

Senate 1 D, 1 R
House 8 D, 3 R

State legislature

Senate 38 D, 12 R
House 74 D, 46 R
Governor James G. Martin, R

At a glance, Democrats appear to have a secure hold on the redistricting process in North Carolina, which may gain a House seat in the 1990s. The Democrats have wide majorities in both houses of the Legislature—38-12 in the Senate (all seats are up in 1990) and 74-46 in the House. And the Legislature has complete control over redistricting legislation. Republican governor James G. Martin is the only governor who lacks the power to veto any legislation. However the situation leading up to the final elections before redistricting is much more complex than these facts indicate.

Although still very much a minority in the Legislature, Republicans have made major progress in Raleigh during the 1980s. Since the 1980 elections, they have built their strength in the state Senate from five to twelve. The net GOP gain of twenty-two seats in the state House—capped by a ten-seat pickup in 1988—has even more significant implications: for the first time in modern North Carolina history, the GOP caucus has more than the one-third vote necessary to prevent legislation from passing without debate under "suspension of the rules."

The Republicans' influence in the Legislature was manifest in the overthrow of veteran Democratic state House Speaker Liston B. Ramsey in January 1989. A solid bloc of House Republicans joined twenty dissident Democrats, who viewed Ramsey as heavy-handed and dictatorial, in a successful effort to elect Democrat Joe Mavretic as Speaker. For their participation in this coalition, Republicans got subcommittee chairmanships.

But no one knows whether this era of bipartisanship will last long enough to diminish Democratic dominance of redistricting in the 1990s. There was striking evidence during the contentious and lengthy 1989 legislative session that the anti-Ramsey coalition was a shaky marriage. (The

1990 session was scheduled to begin May 21).

"The coalition forged between the Republicans and dissident Democrats is extremely fragile," said Thad Beyle, a University of North Carolina political science professor and managing editor of a state political newsletter. For example, an effort to craft a state constitutional amendment giving the governor veto power was tabled in the state House, despite an intense lobbying effort by Governor Martin, who declared in his January 1989 State of the State speech that 1989 would be the "Year of the Veto."

Republican officials say they realize the movement against Ramsey did not constitute a conservative coalition that can be counted on to be sympathetic to Republicans in redistricting. In fact, while there were conservatives in their numbers, the dissidents included some of the state House's most liberal members, who shelved their Democratic partisanship only long enough to dump Ramsey. "[The dissident Democrats] had to do it to help themselves. . . . I don't think they did this because they are really Republicans who just happen to be registered Democrats," said state GOP political director Tim Minton. "They're going to set [redistricting] up in a way that will help the Democrats."

There is also a strong possibility that Ramsey, or one of his fifty-plus loyalists in the House, may attempt to oust Mavretic after the 1990 elections, a prospect that surely does not bode well for Republicans there.

In 1989 the Democratic Legislative Campaign Committee (DLCC), an arm of the state House Democratic caucus, took over the 1990 state House campaign fund raising and targeting effort from the state Democratic party. The DLCC is ostensibly committed to matching the Republicans' aggressive campaign organization and rolling back recent GOP gains. But Mavretic Democrats and Republicans alike worry that the committee will devote much of its effort to electing pro-Ramsey Democrats: House Majority Leader Dennis A. Wicker and his appointee to head the DLCC, state representative Martin L. Nesbitt, are Ramsey supporters, as are most on the DLCC board of directors.

The threat to their new-found standing has provoked North Carolina Republicans to step up their own efforts a notch. The Legislative Forum, which raises campaign funds for Republican state Senate and House candidates, is working in concert with the state GOP's Legislative Candidate Recruitment Committee, which targets mainly challenger races.

The concept of highly organized state legislative campaigns is quite new in North Carolina. "Posters hammered to trees" remain the major campaign medium in a number of state legislative districts, said Republican state representative Robert Grady, who persuaded senior GOP officials to put him in charge of the fledgling state House campaign organization in 1988. While Grady's low-budget, four-person operation was limited to morale-boosting in some districts, it helped bring a level of sophistication, including targeted direct mail, into several key contests. This effort is credited with a role in the big GOP gain that year.

Along with trying to increase their numbers in the Legislature before redistricting, the Republicans are continuing their liaison with black organizations, which have solicited the support of all comers in their efforts to increase black representation. As in some other states, Republicans in North Carolina have supported lawsuits brought by blacks under the Voting Rights Act. These suits challenge at-large districting that gives white Democrats an advantage over blacks and arrangements, mainly in urban areas, that divide black communities among several districts that consistently elect white Democrats.

While black plaintiffs have been able to force redrawing of lines to create majority-black jurisdictions, the remaps also have tended to create mainly white, suburban districts where Republicans can compete. "It allows the black community to choose its own representatives, but it has also helped Republicans," said Grady.

An example of a Republican-black compact occurred during the last congressional redistricting. The original plan passed by the Democrat-dominated Legislature created a 2d District, then held by veteran Democratic representative L. H. Fountain, that was dubbed "Fountain's Fishhook" because it curved carefully around the heavily black city of Durham. But black activists, with the tacit backing of Republicans who were hoping for a better shake in surrounding districts, convinced the U.S. Justice Department that excluding Durham deprived black candidates of a reasonable chance to carry the 2d.

After the Legislature redrew the map, placing Durham in the 2d, Fountain decided to retire. In the first-round 1982 Democratic primary to succeed him, black state representative H. M. "Mickey" Michaux, Jr., finished first but short of the necessary majority. He was then overtaken in the runoff by white Democrat Tim Valentine, who has held the seat since. But the neighboring 4th District, from which Durham was removed, became somewhat more competitive, and was even won by Republican Bill Cobey in 1984. (David E. Price recaptured it for the Democrats in 1986.)

Republican machinations aimed at the next redistricting may be superfluous. Running counter to the national trend of diminished House competition, North Carolina has had an unusual number of marginal districts during the 1980s. Thus, the redistricting process after 1990 could well be a simple line-shifting aimed at bolstering the current incumbents—provided the state holds at eleven House seats.

But if the state gains a seat, as many projections indicate, a major revision of the district lines may indeed ensue. "The whole fruit basket would be upset," said Beyle.

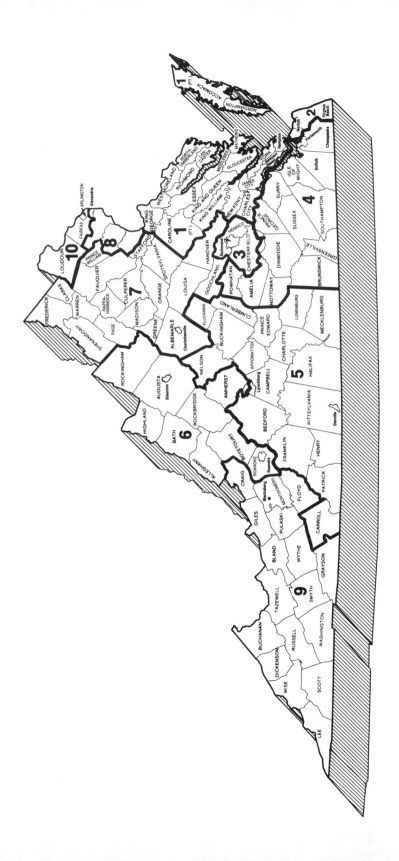

Virginia

Population and growth

1980 population	5,346,818
1989 population estimate	6,098,000
(12th in the nation)	
Percent change 1980-1989	+14%

U.S. Congress

Senate	1 D,	1 R
House	5 D,	5 R

State legislature

Senate	30 D,	10 R	
House	59 D,	39 R,	2 Ind.
Governor	L. Douglas Wilder, D		

With its population growth estimated at more than 14 percent between 1980 and 1989, the Old Dominion now seems certain to gain an eleventh House seat. The fact that there will be Democratic fingerprints on the design of that new district is also beyond question.

Virginia was one of two states to hold legislative elections in 1989 (New Jersey was the other), and Democrats maintained their traditional dominance, with a 59-39-2 edge in the state House and a 30-10 majority in the state Senate. Democratic control of the redistricting process was assured when then-Lt. Gov. L. Douglas Wilder narrowly defeated Republican J. Marshall Coleman in a historic contest that made Wilder the nation's first black elected governor.

Still, these favorable conditions may provide the Democrats more of a bulwark against Republican gains than an opportunity to score a major partisan advantage in the Virginia delegation (which is currently split 5-5 between the parties). Republicans have a good shot at benefiting if the state gains a seat because most of the growth has been in affluent, GOP-leaning D.C. suburbs and in the conservative, defense-oriented Tidewater.

Competition between these regions for a new seat would be stiff. The 8th District, which takes in Washington's outer suburbs in Fairfax and Prince William counties, grew by nearly 17 percent through 1986; the 10th and 7th in Northern Virginia also experienced double-digit growth. However, the 2d District, based in Norfolk and Virginia Beach, grew by almost 15 percent during the same period.

Even with the possible addition of a seat, these areas will likely gain representation at the expense of the state's more rural and economically disadvantaged areas. The 5th District, in Virginia's southern tier, and the 6th and 9th districts, in the mountainous west, grew only a little during the 1980s.

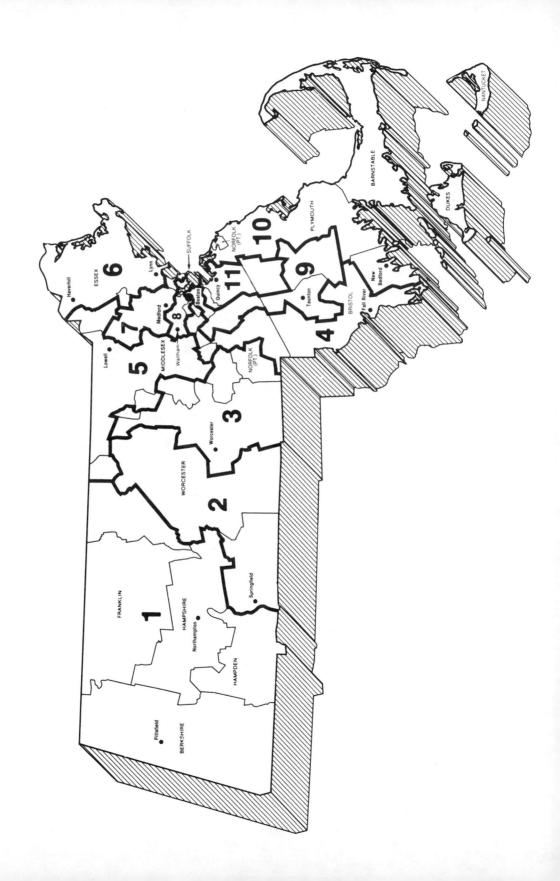

Massachusetts

Population and growth

1980 population	5,737,037
1989 population estimate	5,913,000
(13th in the nation)	
Percent change 1980-1989	+3%

U.S. Congress

Senate 2 D
House 10 D, 1 R

State legislature

Senate 32 D, 8 R
House 128 D, 32 R
Governor Michael S. Dukakis, D

The prospect of losing one House seat for the second consecutive decade has members of the Massachusetts House delegation scrambling. In June 1989 Democratic representative Joe Moakley and GOP representative Silvio O. Conte announced a delegation plan to identify 80,000 new residents of Massachusetts, including students, illegal aliens from Ireland who have sought work in and near Boston, and immigrants from Southeast Asia and Latin America.

Moakley and Conte hope that a full count of these people will enable the state to qualify for the eleven seats it currently holds. But skeptics continue to prepare for a grinding battle over who gets victimized by the one-seat loss that many demographers see as the likelier outcome.

One target of redistricting rumors is Democratic representative Barney Frank, who has been wounded by a scandal involving his relationship with a male prostitute in Washington, D.C. Even if he survives politically, Frank may once again be at the mercy of veteran state legislators who do not have fond memories of his maverick state House tenure in the 1970s. In the last redistricting, the Legislature, though Demo-

crat-dominated, threw Frank into a district that was weighted in favor of Republican representative Margaret M. Heckler (1967-1983); it stretched from Boston's western suburbs to the distant southeastern working-class port of Fall River. But the savvy and aggressive Frank won that 1982 match-up handily, and he has coasted since, even in the 1988 contest that followed his announcement that he is a homosexual. Should Frank win again, no doubt his defenders will try to save his district.

One seemingly obvious geographical target would be the city of Boston. Although its population is barely larger than that of a single House district, Boston is shared by three Democratic members. However, no one expects any in this trio—House Rules Committee Chairman Moakley, Ways and Means member and Irish-issues advocate Brian Donnelly, or Massachusetts political scion Joseph P. Kennedy II—to yield ground. Nor will relatively senior members such as Edward J. Markey and Nicholas Mavroules, or state Democratic party chairman Chester G. Atkins, all suburban Democrats bolstered by their reach into the blue-collar towns and liberal outposts near Boston.

Republicans, who have only Conte's 1st District in western Massachusetts, will likely argue for a major reshaping of the Boston-area district map, hoping to improve their prospects of winning a suburban seat.

The GOP will, as usual, have little impact in the Legislature, where Democrats reign with majorities of 32-8 in the Senate and 128-32 in the House. But the Republicans have some chance of capturing the third leg of the redistricting tripod: the governor's office being vacated by retiring Democrat Michael S. Dukakis. His plummet in popularity, brought on by his 1988 presidential loss and an ensuing state budget crisis, is seen as a burden for the Democratic nominee to succeed him.

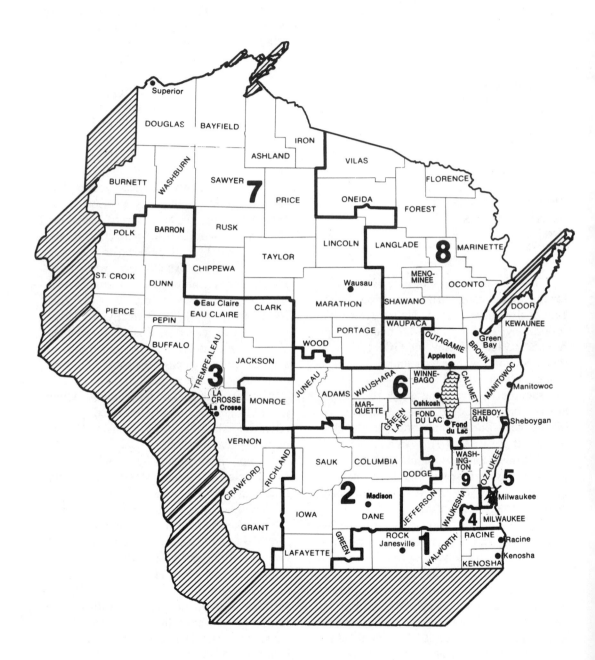

Wisconsin

Population and growth

1980 population	4,705,767
1989 population estimate	4,867,000
(17th in the nation)	
Percent change 1980-1989	+3%

U.S. Congress

Senate	1 D,	1 R
House	5 D,	4 R

State legislature

Senate	19 D,	14 R	
House	55 D,	42 R,	2 Vacancies
Governor	Tommy G. Thompson, R		

With a population increase of just over 3 percent between 1980 and 1989, Wisconsin is another borderline prospect for a one-seat loss. Based on census figures, that possibility would appear most troublesome to the Democrats in the southeastern districts—the 1st (Armed Services Committee Chairman Les Aspin), 4th (Gerald D. Kleczka), and 5th (Jim Moody)—which lost an estimated 1 percent to 4 percent of their residents through 1986.

However, political realities put these Democrats on firmer footing. Their party controls the state Legislature, with an 19-14 margin in the Senate and a 55-42 (with two vacancies) edge in the Assembly.

Although these majorities are not so huge as to be insurmountable for the Republicans, the recent trend in legislative elections has not been toward the GOP. The Democrats gained one state Senate and two Assembly seats not only in 1988, when Democrat Michael S. Dukakis carried the state for president, but also in 1986, when Republican Tommy G. Thompson won the governorship.

At this point, Thompson provides a bulwark against Democratic redistricting

mischief aimed at the state's four GOP House members. In 1981, when a similar situation prevailed, Republican governor Lee Sherman Dreyfus blocked a plan drawn by the Democratic-controlled Legislature that would have placed Republicans Toby Roth and Thomas E. Petri in the same district, while also doing harm to GOP representative Steve Gunderson.

But even though Thompson looks strong entering his 1990 reelection campaign, wary state Republicans are supporting a proposal to get the Legislature out of the line-drawing business.

In August 1989 the state Republican Executive Committee passed a resolution calling for the creation of an independent commission to redraw the congressional and state legislative district maps for the 1990s.

The Republicans couch their proposal in the usual "good government" vernacular. They are also making a strong appeal to black activists by promising that the commission plan would "maximize minority representation in the [state] legislature."

Democratic leaders, here and elsewhere, deride such appeals as ploys to concentrate minority voters in a few inner-city districts while improving Republican chances in ethnic-urban and suburban areas. However, some black officials regard increased black political opportunity as a higher priority than protecting Democratic majorities; they may be receptive to the GOP argument. "My interest lies with whoever can strengthen and empower African Americans," Democratic state representative Annette Polly Williams has said.

In any case, this issue in Wisconsin has much more to do with redistricting for the state Legislature than for Congress. It would be impossible to fashion a majority-black U.S. House district in Wisconsin: even in Milwaukee's 5th District, where blacks are heavily concentrated, they make up less than 30 percent of the population.

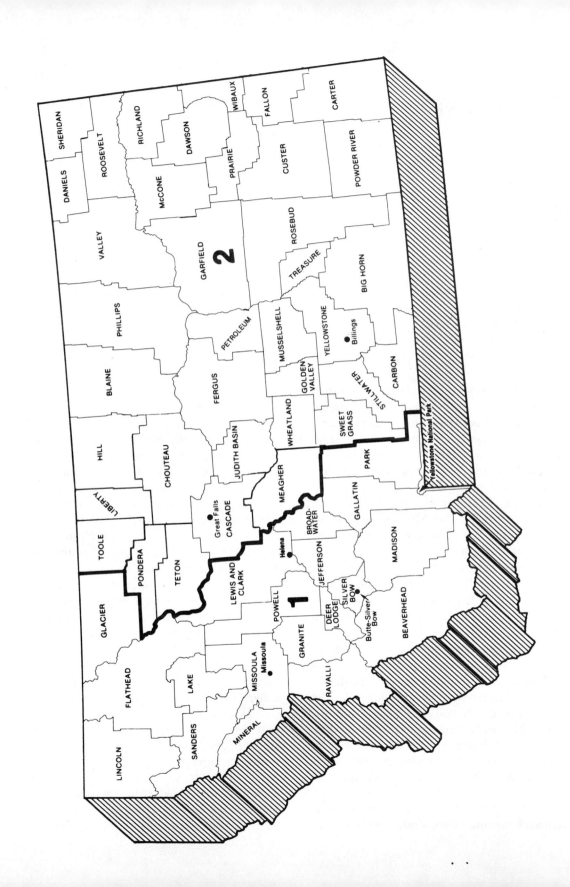

Montana

Population and growth

1980 population	786,690
1989 population estimate	806,000
(44th in the nation)	
Percent change 1980-1989	+2%

U.S. Congress

Senate	1 D,	1 R
House	1 D,	1 R

State legislature

Senate	23 D,	27 R
House	52 D,	48 R
Governor	Stan Stephens, R	

Montana has a law mandating a bipartisan commission to handle congressional redistricting, one of only five states with such a structure. However, Montana's board will probably not even have to be established in the 1990s: most projections indicate that the state—whose population increased an estimated 2 percent between 1980 and 1989—will lose one of its two House seats.

That occurence would render redistricting unnecessary. It could also set up a fierce battle between Democratic representative Pat Williams and GOP representative Ron Marlenee—if the two chose to face off for the at-large seat.

If the state is able to hold on to its two seats, the redistricting commission will likely have to make few changes in what Montanans call the "Western District" (Williams's 1st) and the "Eastern District" (Marlenee's 2d). The 1986 Census Bureau population estimates showed a difference of fewer than 3,000 residents between the districts, with the 1st holding the edge.

The houses of the Montana Legislature moved in opposite partisan directions in the 1988 election. A two-seat state Senate gain for the Republicans moved them from a 25-25 tie to a 27-23 majority (half of the Senate seats are up in 1990). A three-seat gain by the state House Democrats enabled them to move from a 49-51 deficit to a 52-48 majority.

But the Legislature has no role in congressional redistricting in any case. The five-member commission bears total responsibility for crafting a plan, which is then sent directly to the Montana secretary of state for publication.

8

States Not Changing

Although not projected to gain or lose U.S. House seats after the 1990 census, the twenty-six other multidistrict states still have to redraw their lines to adjust for population variances among districts that have developed during the past decade. The outcome of legislative campaigns in these states will be a factor in determining the degree of partisanship in congressional redistricting.

New Jersey

Population and growth

1980 population	7,364,823
1989 population estimate	7,763,000
(9th in the nation)	
Percent change 1980-1989	+5%

U.S. Congress

Senate 2 D
House 7 D, 6 R, 1 Vacancy

State legislature

Senate 23 D, 17 R
House 44 D, 36 R
Governor Jim Florio, D

Redistricting politics have come full circle for New Jersey's Democrats, who dominated state government in the early 1980s, lost their grip on power for most of the decade, then regained it just in time for the 1990's remap.

Voters in New Jersey—one of only two states (Virginia was the other) to hold statewide elections in 1989—elected Democratic representative Jim Florio by a wide margin to succeed Republican governor Thomas H. Kean, who had to retire after two-terms. Florio overwhelmed GOP representative Jim Courter, winning with 61 percent of the vote.

Florio's coattails also helped restore the Democrats' control of the state House, which had been lost in Kean's reelection landslide four years earlier. The Democrats' five-seat gain in 1989 gave them a 44-36 majority in the state House to go with their 23-17 edge in the state Senate (which had no regularly scheduled elections that year). With Florio in place as governor, the Democrats will control all legs of the redistricting "tripod" when the process begins in 1991.

The degree of change required in the congressional redistricting—and the amount of latitude for Democratic partisan craftsmanship—depends largely on whether New Jersey, whose estimated population increased by 5 percent between 1980 and 1989, loses a House seat. If the state holds on to all fourteen seats, as many population

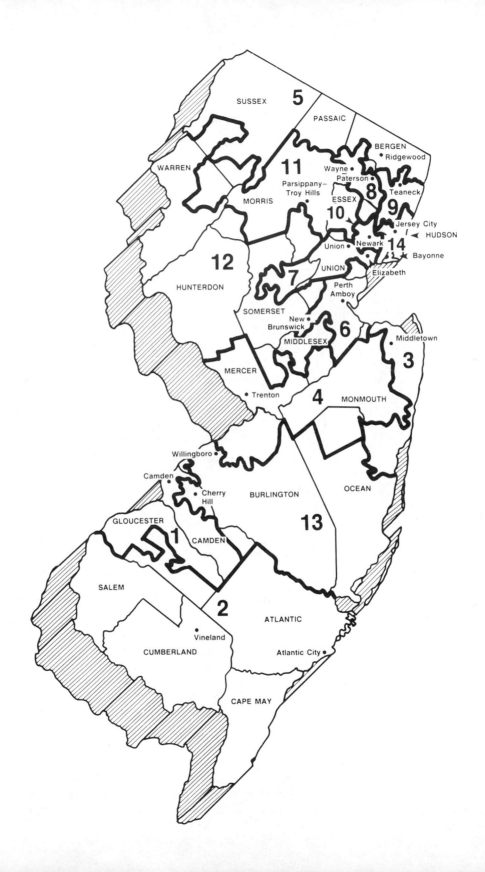

analysts predict, the lines will require some undramatic tinkering. Variations between districts have developed over the decade, with slight population declines in the urbanized areas near New York City offset by sizable upswings in suburban/exurban districts such as the 4th, the 12th, and the 13th. But the loss of a seat would mandate a major map overhaul, setting the stage for a partisan war similar to that which occurred in the 1980s redistricting.

State Republicans have valid reasons for concern about the Democratic control of the redistricting process, given the Democrats' artful map drawing when they ran the show in 1981. That year's plan, passed by the Democratic majorities in both houses of the Legislature and signed by Democratic governor Brendan T. Byrne, dismembered the district of Republican representative Millicent Fenwick (then planning her 1982 Senate campaign) to compensate for the one-seat loss. It also redrew the lines so GOP representatives Courter and Marge Roukema would be paired in the 5th District. In addition, Republican Matthew J. Rinaldo's home was placed in the suburban/exurban 12th District, seemingly opening the 7th District's urban areas, which he had represented, for a Democratic takeover.

The erratic lines in the Democratic remap—including an ungainly stretch from the New York suburbs westward to the Delaware River that was dubbed "the Swan"—inspired comparisons with the controversial California plan of that period. But the Democrats' handiwork was soon undone. Courter moved to the 12th, avoiding a fight with Roukema, while Rinaldo shifted to and held the 7th. Then, in 1983, the U.S. Supreme Court ruled in the Republicans' favor in *Karcher v. Daggett*, voiding the congressional map on the basis of unequal populations between districts. (The decision firmly established near-exact population equality as a paramount criterion for redistricting plans.)

The district map, redrawn for the 1984 elections, removed some of the more extreme contortions of the original plan. It also moved 11th District Democratic representative Joseph G. Minish farther into the suburbs, where he lost in 1984 to Republican Dean A. Gallo.

Although redistricting was a priority concern for New Jersey political insiders in 1989, it was an nonissue for most voters, who instead focused on the then-raging debate over abortion. In the wake of the Supreme Court's decision in *Webster v. Reproductive Health Services,* Florio took a staunch pro-abortion rights position and galvanized the support of activists who shared those views. Courter, who had previously been regarded as anti-abortion, hedged on the issue, infuriating the conservative wing of the New Jersey GOP and enabling Florio to accuse Courter of "waffling."

Florio's ability to gain the initiative on the abortion issue gave him a leg up in a campaign that resulted in an easy victory. Several Democratic candidates who also had the assistance of pro-abortion rights organizations won state House races, aiding the party's efforts to win the majority in that body.

On the other hand, the abortion issue derailed Courter's political career. In February 1990 Courter announced that, after serious thought, he had come to support a woman's right to choose abortion. But after his statement further alienated conservatives who were once his most loyal supporters and sparked another round of media stories about his 1989 indecision on the issue, Courter announced he would not run for a seventh House term in 1990.

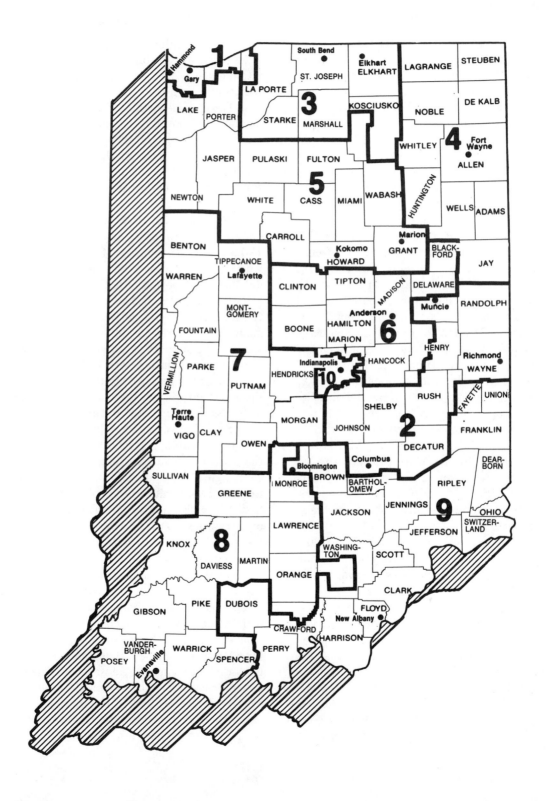

Indiana

Population and growth

1980 population	5,490,224
1989 population estimate	5,593,000
(14th in the nation)	
Percent change 1980-1989	+2%

U.S. Congress

Senate 2 R
House 7 D, 3 R

State legislature

Senate 24 D, 26 R
House 49 D, 51 R
Governor Evan Bayh, D

The projections for Indiana's congressional redistricting portend little drama: unlike in the post-1980 round, Indiana is not expected to lose a seat, and population variations among the state's ten districts are not great.

But few familiar with Indiana politics doubt the potential for partisan craftsmanship when lines are redrawn. Indiana was the scene of the most famous—albeit ultimately unsuccessful—GOP gerrymander in the 1980s. This fact is not lost on the Democrats, who hold the governorship and will be fighting in 1990 for control of the one of the most evenly divided Legislatures in the nation.

The 1988 elections left the once-dominant state Republicans with a slim 26-24 edge in the Senate and an unprecedented 50-50 split in the House that required an arrangement under which Democratic leader Michael K. Phillips and Republican Paul S. Mannweiler alternated daily as Speaker. However, the balance shifted back to the GOP in late February 1990, when antiabortion Democratic state representative Frank Newkirk switched parties, giving the Republicans a 51-49 edge.

Still, these narrow Republican advantages have aroused Democratic hopes of capturing one or both houses of the Legislature in time for the 1990s congressional and legislative district remaps. Such a concept would have been rejected as zany in the aftermath of the 1980s' redistricting.

Boosted by the 1980 Reagan landslide, Indiana Republicans ran up huge margins of 35-15 in the Senate and 63-37 in the House. Those majorities appeared to have been cemented before the 1982 elections by a GOP-gerrymandered legislative district map so despised by Democrats that they fought it all the way to the Supreme Court, in the case of *Davis v. Bandemer.*

Yet a gradual Democratic comeback culminated in a quantum leap in the 1988 elections. Led by gubernatorial candidate Evan Bayh—whose victory ended the GOP's twenty-year hold on the state's top job—Indiana Democrats gained two seats to draw temporarily even in the House and picked up four seats in the Senate. These gains occurred even as George Bush and native son Dan Quayle were winning 60 percent at the top of the GOP ticket.

With the recent Republican slippage in the Legislature, what had been regarded as one of the most infamous gerrymanders of the 1980s is now seen as one of the decade's political flops. A similar conclusion had been reached much earlier about the Republican-drawn congressional map, which in 1982 was being compared to California's as an example of partisan art. The Republicans managed to merge two Democratic districts to compensate for the state's one-seat loss. But their hopes of dominating the House delegation were dashed. From a 5-5 split after 1982, Democrats have gained a 7-3 majority.

In the Legislature, the Democrats' resurgence has come despite a district map that the party argued was inalterably biased. It was in the 1986 decision in the

Bandemer case that the Supreme Court stated for the first time that the courts could examine the effects of redistricting on partisan communities-of-interest as evidence of gerrymandering. However, the Court ruled that the Indiana map did not meet its still-vague definition of a political gerrymander.

Today, Democratic officials deny that their revival undercuts their charges of gerrymandering. But some Democrats say the map actually contributed to the Republicans' predicament. During the remap, the swollen ranks of GOP incumbents—many of them newly elected in marginal areas—clamored for security. "They tried to create thirty safe districts," said state senator Louis J. Mahern, Jr., the assistant Democratic floor leader. "They cut them too fine."

Democrats say the gerrymander also spurred them to reinvigorate the candidate-recruiting and fund-raising efforts of the Senate and House legislative caucuses. Democrats developed a highly targeted effort. "Republicans running in safe districts will scream if the PACs [political action committees] don't give as much money as in very competitive districts," said Bob Bales, public affairs associate for the Indiana-based, GOP-oriented Eli Lilly pharmaceutical company. "The Democrats tell safe incumbents to run on their own."

In addition, Democrats have benefited from the aggressive efforts of Democratic-oriented lobbying groups, such as the Indiana State Teachers' Association (ISTA), to topple some of the Legislature's leading conservatives. In 1986 ISTA helped defeat GOP House Speaker J. Roberts Dailey.

Leading officials in both parties agree on one point: through 1988 Republicans suffered from complacency and public weariness. "We were able to capitalize on the feeling that maybe the Republicans were in power for too long," said Mahern. Said L. Keith Bulen, a former Republican state chairman who has been brought back to run the party's legislative campaign operation in 1990: "The state government gets some barnacles."

Although the battles for the legislative majorities are clearly important to the direction of state policy, the redistricting implications, at least at the congressional level, are not as daunting as in 1980. In addition, Democrats are seeking to assure voters that they will not use the redistricting pen as a scalpel if they gain control of the process.

The return of Bulen, referred to in an *Indianapolis Star* article as "the architect of the modern Indiana Republican Party" during a tenure that began in the late 1960s, suggests a more aggressive posture for the GOP. Bulen, chairman of the party's "Victory '90" organization, is coordinating the campaign efforts of the state party, the House and Senate Republican caucuses, and the Republican National Committee, which has taken a strong pre-redistricting interest in Indiana's situation.

Washington

Population and growth

1980 population	4,132,156
1989 population estimate	4,761,000
(18th in the nation)	
Percent change 1980-1989	+15%

U.S. Congress

Senate   1 D,   1 R
House   5 D,   3 R

State legislature

Senate   24 D,   25 R
House   63 D,   35 R
Governor   Booth Gardner, D

With its tradition of mild partisanship, open primaries, and "good government" experimentation, it is not surprising that Washington is one of a handful of states to create a congressional redistricting mechanism aimed at limiting the role of politics.

Under a state constitutional amendment the Legislature passed and voters approved in 1983, a five-member commission will draw Washington's congressional map. Legislators will eventually have a limited say in the process, but the new map is expected to be enacted largely as minted by the commission.

The congressional redistricting commission will include four voting members, with one appointed by each of the state legislative party caucuses (the law bars legislators and their staff from being appointees). These four will choose a nonvoting chairman to preside over deliberations.

Washington's redistricting process will certainly be one of the most open in the nation: anyone with the inclination—individuals, parties, legislators, and other political actors—may submit a remap proposal to the commission. The Legislature is procuring computer equipment and setting up a redistricting database, to be in the secretary of state's office, for interested parties to use.

Once the commission completes its plan, the Legislature will debate it. However, the law provides little leeway for partisan-minded legislators to tinker: in changing the plan, no more than 2 percent of any district's population can be moved, and overall district population-equality goals must be respected.

The even Democrat-Republican split among voting members on the redistricting commission, along with the Legislature's role in the process, creates the potential for stalemate. But most expect the law's bipartisan intent to be respected.

Demographics may allow this goal to be met rather easily. Although the state's estimated 15 percent population increase from 1980 to 1989 gives it an outside chance for an additional House seat, most projections show Washington holding at eight seats after 1990.

If this situation prevails, remapping will require relatively minor shifts of population from rapidly developing districts in suburban-exurban Seattle—including the Republican-held 8th and 1st and the Democratic 2d and 6th—to slower-growth venues such as House Speaker Thomas S. Foley's 5th District in eastern Washington, the Republican 4th in the central part of the state, and the Democratic 7th in urban Seattle.

The expected calm next time would be in sharp contrast with the situation after the 1980 census. The state's then-surging population had earned it a new House seat, requiring a major map renovation. This opportunity spurred an aggressive—and successful—GOP effort to win the governorship and control of both houses of the Legislature.

Then-GOP governor John D. Spellman vetoed an initial remap plan weakening one

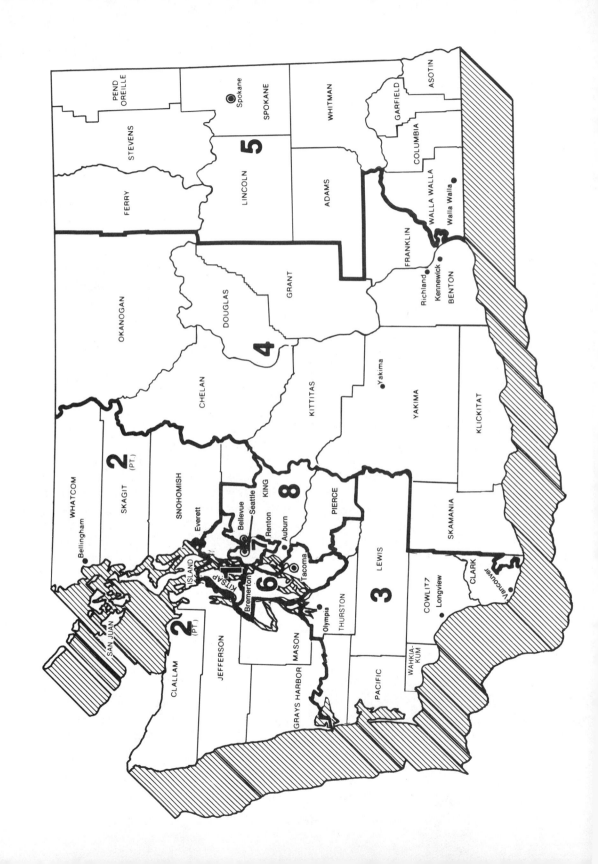

incumbent in each party. The Legislature then approved a map under which all seven House incumbents, including five Democrats, were reelected handily. The dominant GOP crafted the new 8th District (east and south of Seattle) to elect a Republican, which it did.

Still, this map met with opposition that eventually brought its rejection by a federal district court on population-inequality grounds after the 1982 elections. The dispute was parochial rather than political: residents of Everett opposed shifting their city to the 1st District from its traditional home in the 2d. The Legislature shifted the city back in 1983 map alterations that had no partisan repercussions.

But the fact that even a relatively mild redistricting plan could not survive judicial review boosted the movement for a redistricting commission. Promoters of the commission idea also said removing remapping from the Legislature's control would temper the partisanship in legislative elections before redistricting. A GOP offensive led to a fourteen-seat state House gain in 1978 and a seven-seat 1980 pickup that gave Republicans a 56-42 majority (to go with their 25-24 Senate edge).

The Republicans' lock after 1980 let them dominate legislative as well as congressional redistricting. However, any GOP advantage in the state House remap was wiped out in its first test by a Democratic tide that has strengthened through the 1980s. Democrats regained a 54-44 House edge in 1982 and now hold a 63-35 majority.

Democrats say the Republicans' state House gerrymander boomeranged. "Individual Republicans began to ask for a little here, a little there," said Jeff Smith, executive director of the state Democratic party. "They cut it a bit too fine."

The Republican remap of Senate districts managed at least to maintain the long-term, tenuous balance in that body. Majority control has seesawed through the 1980s. Democrats took a 25-24 edge in 1982, gained to 27-22 seats in 1984, then slipped back to 25-24 in 1986. In 1987 Republicans won a special election in a formerly Democratic district, returning the GOP to a 25-24 majority. That one-seat edge was preserved in 1988, despite a Democratic presidential win and a gubernatorial landslide in the state.

With one seat making the difference in the Senate, two aggressive party caucus campaign organizations going at each other, and no statewide contests on the ballot, the Senate elections may take center stage in 1990—even without the redistricting issue to fuel the fire.

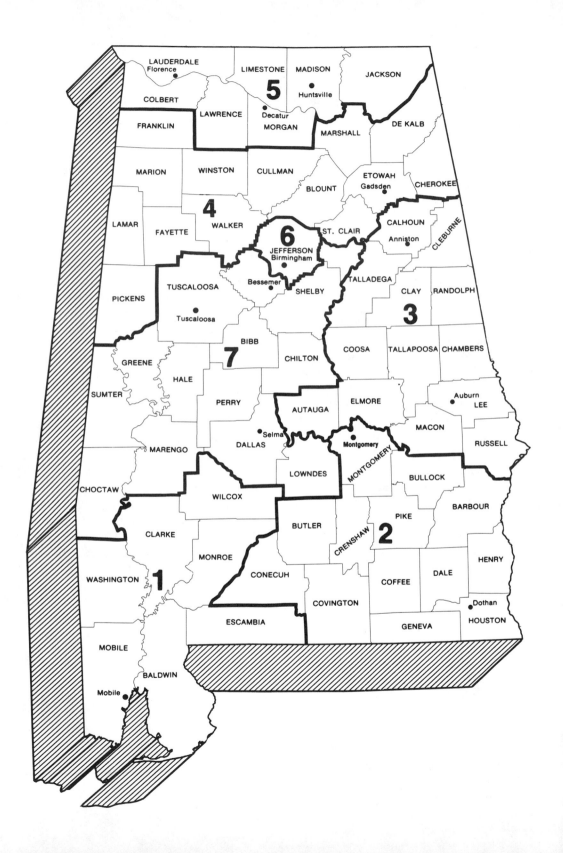

Alabama

Population and growth

1980 population	3,893,888
1989 population estimate	4,118,000
(22d in the nation)	
Percent change 1980-1989	+6%

U.S. Congress

Senate   2 D
House   5 D,   2 R

State legislature

Senate   27 D,   8 R
House   83 D,   22 R
Governor Guy Hunt, R

Still searching for a larger share of the Sun Belt development boom, Alabama has seen only modest population growth in the 1980s and is expected to hold at seven House seats. As usual, a Democratic-controlled Legislature will redraw lines after 1990. But there may be a very different player in the process: GOP governor Guy Hunt, the first Republican to hold the office since the nineteenth century.

Unlike ten years ago—when there were no Republicans in the Senate and only four in the House—the GOP has a beachhead in both chambers. Nonetheless, Democrats still thoroughly dominate, by 27-8 in the Senate (where all seats are up in 1990) and 83-22 in the House.

Hunt, if reelected in 1990, would provide Republicans with a check on any map-making mischief by the Legislature's Democrats. But recent remaps in Alabama have tended not to be very partisan anyway, with the interests of both Democratic and Republican incumbents protected.

The only member who would appear to have even mild redistricting concerns is Democrat Ben Erdreich. His 6th District (Birmingham), with its sagging steel industry, lost a few thousand residents from 1980 to 1986; a farther reach into the suburbs could bring more Republican voters into his territory.

The northern Alabama 5th (Huntsville), held by Democratic representative Ronnie G. Flippo, a 1990 gubernatorial hopeful, has grown by an estimated 10 percent and will have to shed some excess population.

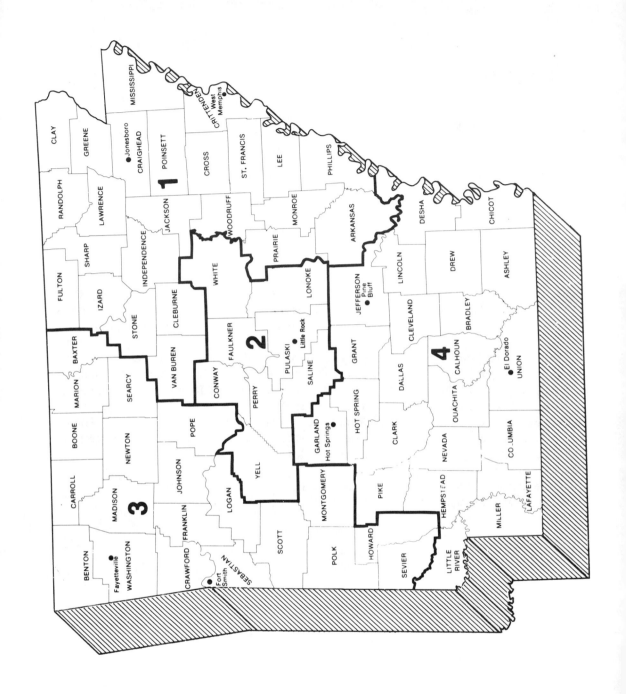

Arkansas

Population and growth

1980 population	2,286,435
1989 population estimate	2,406,000
(33d in the nation)	
Percent change 1980-1989	+5%

U.S. Congress

Senate 2 D
House 2 D, 2 R

State legislature

Senate 31 D, 4 R
House 88 D, 11 R, 1 Ind.
Governor Bill Clinton, D

With its population up by just 5 percent through 1989, Arkansas is expected to stay at four House seats for the fourth straight decade. Relatively minor changes, requiring the shift of a handful of counties among districts, are likely. The faster-growing districts—the 3d (up by 8 percent in the 1986 Census Bureau estimates), represented by Republican John Paul Hammer-schmidt, and the Little Rock-based 2d (up by 6 percent), held by recent GOP party-switcher and 1990 gubernatorial candidate Tommy F. Robinson—will have to give some residents to the flat-growth 1st and 4th, bailiwicks of Democrats Bill Alexander and Beryl Anthony, Jr.

Democrats hold massive majorities in both houses of the Legislature: 31-4 in the Senate and 88-11-1 in the House. The Democrats will control the redistricting process: Gov. Bill Clinton is seeking reelection, and polls show him a likely winner.

After the 1980 census, redistricting control was divided between the Democratic Legislature and GOP governor Frank White. A relatively unpartisan plan sailed through to passage in June 1981, making Arkansas the first state to approve a House remap.

But the next January, it also became the first state to have its plan voided by a federal district court on the ground of population inequality (a 2 percent variation between the largest and smallest districts). The court quickly accepted a new plan with minor changes and no partisan impact.

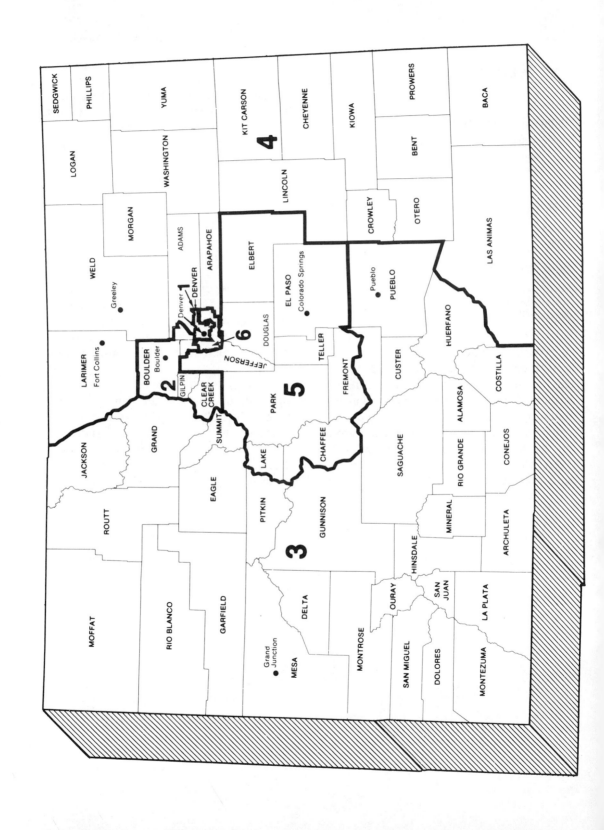

Colorado

Population and growth

1980 population	2,889,964
1989 population estimate	3,317,000
(26th in the nation)	
Percent change 1980-1989	+15%

U.S. Congress

Senate	1 D, 1 R
House	3 D, 3 R

State legislature

Senate	11 D, 24 R
House	26 D, 39 R
Governor	Roy Romer, D

Although Colorado's estimated population was up by 15 percent through mid-1989, the state's land rush has moderated to the point that it is unlikely to gain a House seat. The 1990s therefore will mark the first decade since the 1960s in which Colorado did not gain a House seat. But an imbalance in growth within the state will necessitate a fairly major redrawing of the lines.

The 5th (Colorado Springs), a defense-oriented district held by Republican Joel Hefley, and the 6th, the affluent suburban Denver district of Republican Dan Schaefer, both grew by more than 20 percent from 1980 to 1986 (each increased its population by more than 100,000); Democrat David E. Skaggs's 2d District, which takes in Denver's northern suburbs and the university city of Boulder, was up by 14 percent.

Some of these districts' residents will have to be shifted to slower-growth constituencies, including western Colorado's 3d District (up by 7 percent), represented by Democrat Ben Nighthorse Campbell, and Democrat Patricia Schroeder's 1st (up by only 2 percent), which encompasses Denver. Eastern Colorado's 4th District, which also grew modestly in the 1980s, will have a freshman member at the time of redistricting; Republican incumbent Hank Brown is running for the seat being vacated by GOP senator William L. Armstrong.

Republican control of the Legislature seems secure, with majorities of 24-11 in the Senate (half the seats are up in 1990) and 39-26 in the House. The media in Colorado have picked up on Republican ruminations about the redistricting damage that could be done to incumbent Democrats, especially Schroeder. But any gerrymandering attempt would bump into a mighty obstacle: popular Democratic governor Roy Romer, who appears well positioned for reelection in 1990.

A similar split occurred after the 1980 census, which boosted the state from five to six House seats. The Republican-controlled Legislature passed three plans, all of which would likely have created a 4-2 Republican edge in the delegation. However, Democratic governor Richard D. Lamm vetoed all three. Finally, the remap fell to a federal district court panel, whose plan resulted in a 3-3 split that has been rather sturdy. Only the 3d District has changed hands during the 1980s, going from Democratic to Republican in 1984 and back in 1986.

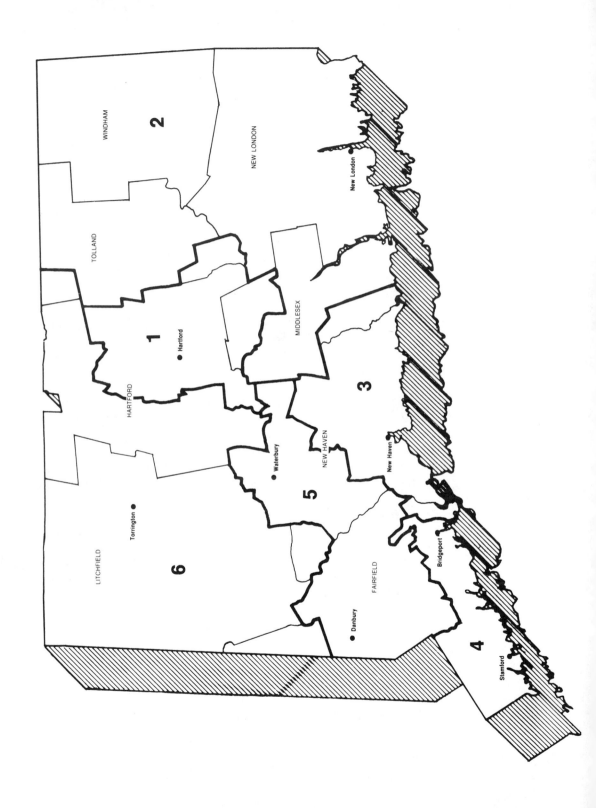

Connecticut

Population and growth

1980 population	3,107,576
1989 population estimate	3,239,000
(28th in the nation)	
Percent change 1980-1989	+4%

U.S. Congress

Senate 2 D
House 3 D, 3 R

State legislature

Senate 23 D, 13 R
House 88 D, 63 R
Governor William A. O'Neill, D

With Connecticut likely to hold at six House seats in the 1990s, there may not be much spice to congressional redistricting. Redrawing the district lines will be turned over to an eight-member committee appointed in equal numbers by the Democratic and Republican leaders of the Legislature. Members of the Legislature will have a say over the commission plan, which must pass by a two-thirds majority. But if that fails, a nine-member commission, with total control over the process, will draw up the final revisions.

Even without the commission setup, the Democrats, who control both the Legislature and the governorship, might find it difficult to justify a major revamp. The 1986 Census Bureau estimate found a variation of only 35,000 residents between the least- and most-populous districts. And the slower-growing districts are adjacent to more robust districts currently held by members of the same party.

Republican Christopher Shays's 4th District, a region of affluent suburbs and aging industrial cities that lost just a little over 1 percent of its residents through 1986, borders on the modestly growing 5th and 6th of Republicans Nancy L. Johnson and John G. Rowland. Similarly, Democrat Sam Gejdenson's 2d District may be able to share a few thousand residents with the 1st and the 3d, held by Democrats Barbara B. Kennelly and Bruce A. Morrison.

This partisan balance could be upset by the 1990 gubernatorial contest, however. Rowland and Morrison announced plans early in the year to vacate their House seats and run for governor.

Democrats appear likely to maintain their control over the Legislature through the redistricting period: they lead by 23-13 in the Senate and by 88-63 in the House. Despite a 52 percent presidential victory for longtime Connecticut resident George Bush in 1988, Republicans gained only two seats in the Senate and three in the House.

This outcome is partly attributable to the elimination of the party-line lever option in Connecticut balloting. As late as the mid-1980s the state was susceptible to major party swings in its Legislature. In 1984 the Reagan landslide vaulted Republicans into legislative control, with gains of eleven seats in the Senate and twenty-three in the House. But the Democrats, aided by a big reelection win by Democratic governor William A. O'Neill, rebounded in 1986, gaining fourteen seats in the Senate and twenty-seven in the House.

O'Neill's popularity slipped sharply in ensuing years, as the state government struggled with the fiscal consequences of the economic slowdown affecting Connecticut and other northeastern states. In March 1990 O'Neill announced he would not seek reelection, putting Morrison in the driver's seat for the Democratic nomination.

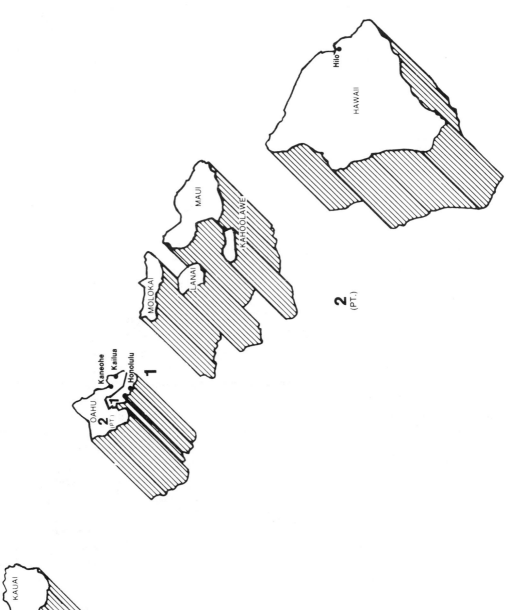

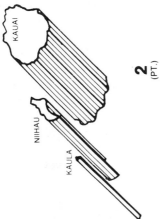

Hawaii

Population and growth

1980 population	964,691
1989 population estimate	1,112,000
(39th in the nation)	
Percent change 1980-1989	+15%

U.S. Congress

Senate   2 D
House   1 D,   1 R

State legislature

Senate   22 D,   3 R
House   45 D,   6 R
Governor   John Waihee III, D

Hawaii's congressional remap requires adjusting only a single line separating the state's two House districts. Yet the state is one of five to turn its congressional redistricting over to a commission.

In fact, redistricting in Hawaii is almost totally independent of the regular legislative process. Members of the commission are appointed by the Legislature's Democratic and GOP leaders, but they have complete control over the redistricting plan, which is submitted to neither the governor nor the full Legislature for approval.

The existence of this bipartisan panel is probably comforting to Rep. Patricia Saiki, who in 1986 became the first Republican elected to the House from Hawaii. If redistricting were conducted by the full Legislature, the design of Saiki's Honolulu-based 1st District would be in the hands of a Senate (half of whose seats are up in 1990) that has a 22-3 Democratic majority and a House with a 45-6 Democratic margin. Gov. John Waihee III, a Democrat, is up for reelection in 1990.

Still, if demographic trends hold up, Saiki's district will have to absorb thousands of residents from the faster-growing 2d District, represented by Democrat Daniel K. Akaka. The 1986 Census Bureau estimates showed the 2d bounding ahead with a 16 percent population increase, while the 1st grew by barely 4 percent.

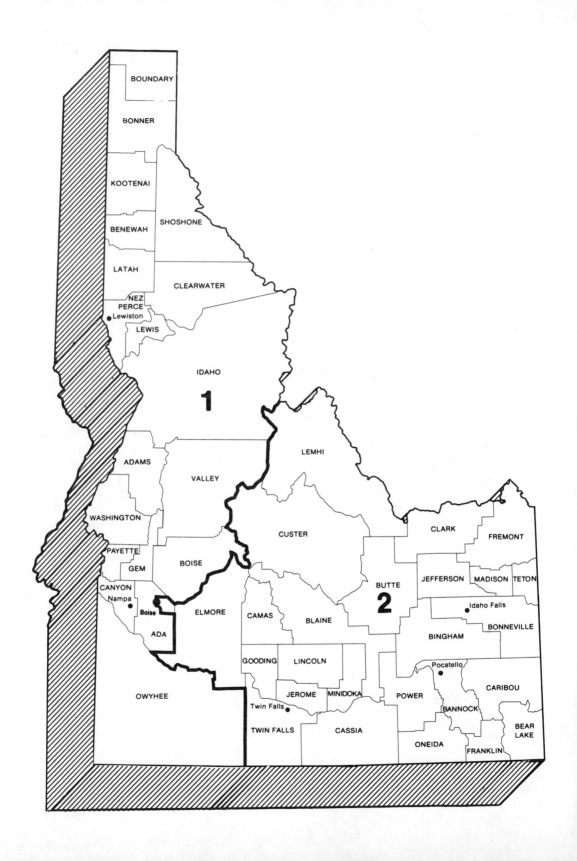

Idaho

Population and growth

1980 population	943,935
1989 population estimate	1,014,000
(42d in the nation)	
Percent change 1980-1989	+7%

U.S. Congress

Senate	2 R
House	1 D, 1 R

State legislature

Senate	18 D,	24 R
House	21 D,	63 R
Governor	Cecil D. Andrus, D	

Idaho is one of the few states in which the 1990 legislative elections may not be decisive for redistricting: although the remap could be done sooner, the Legislature may not deal with it until its 1993 session. The population scenario appears to provide little potential for redistricting dramatics in any case. Modest growth has sent Idaho's population over 1 million for the first time, but the state will have only two seats.

Idaho's growth patterns do not lend themselves to major changes in the line that divides the districts. The 1986 Census Bureau population estimates showed a difference of just 6,600 people between Republican Larry E. Craig's 1st District and Democrat Richard Stallings's 2d. (Craig is running in 1990 to succeed retiring Republican senator James A. McClure.)

The GOP, with majorities of 24-18 in the Senate (all members are up in 1990) and 63-21 in the House, would undoubtedly prefer to make life more difficult for Stallings, who has won three terms in the otherwise GOP-oriented 2d District in eastern Idaho. But prospects for GOP gerrymandering will be parried if Democrats hold the governorship.

Cecil D. Andrus won the office narrowly in 1986 but appears on solid ground as he prepares for his expected 1990 bid. The point may be rendered moot, anyway, if Stallings gives up his House seat in 1992 to challenge Republican senator Steve Symms, a possibility that has been often discussed.

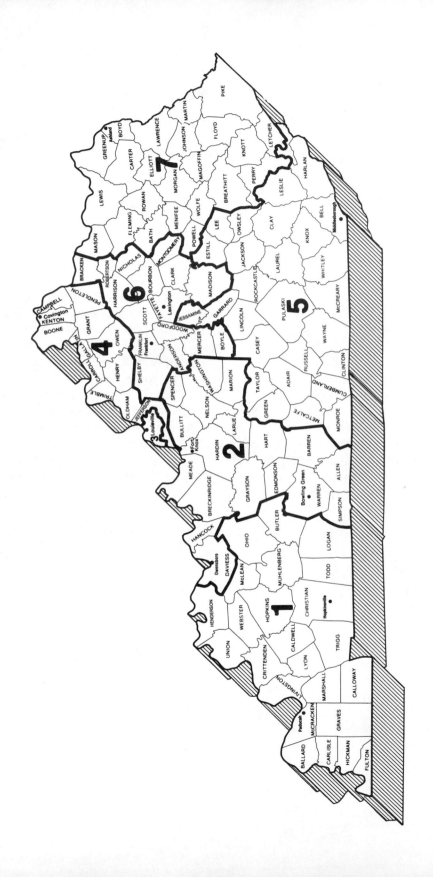

Kentucky

Population and growth

1980 population	3,660,777
1989 population estimate	3,727,000
(23d in the nation)	
Percent change 1980-1989	+2%

U.S. Congress

Senate	1 D,	1 R
House	4 D,	3 R

State legislature

Senate	30 D,	8 R
House	71 D,	29 R
Governor	Wallace G. Wilkinson, D	

The 1990 state legislative campaign in Kentucky is likely to be a low-key affair. The solid Democratic control of both houses of the Legislature—30-8 in the Senate (half the seats are up in 1990) and 71-29 in the House—militates against the urgency of what could be the final elections before redistricting (although state law allows remapping to carry into 1993, if necessary).

The Democrats are also assured of control of the governorship going into the next round of redistricting. Gov. Wallace G. Wilkinson was elected to a four-year term in 1987.

While Democrats appear to have a lock on all three legs of the process, recent congressional remaps indicate that Republicans do not have much to worry about. The Democrats similarly dominated the process after the 1980 census, but the changes in the state's seven districts had no impact on the prevailing balance in the House delegation, four Democrats and three Republicans.

The districts' partisan tendencies were constant throughout the 1980s. None of the districts switched parties during that period, and only two of the faces changed; Democrat Carl C. Perkins succeeded his late father, 7th District representative Carl D. Perkins, in 1984, and GOP representative Gene Snyder retired and turned the 4th District over to Republican Jim Bunning in 1987. The five other incumbents—Democrats Carroll Hubbard, Jr., William H. Natcher, and Romano L. Mazzoli and Republicans Harold Rogers and Larry J. Hopkins—were in office at the last redistricting.

Few adjustments appear necessary in the Kentucky map, anyway. Hubbard's 1st District (far western Kentucky) and Mazzoli's 3d (Louisville) lost about 2 percent of their residents from 1980 to 1986. But they will likely be able to claim some of the surplus population in Natcher's 2d District, which had an estimated growth rate of 5 percent.

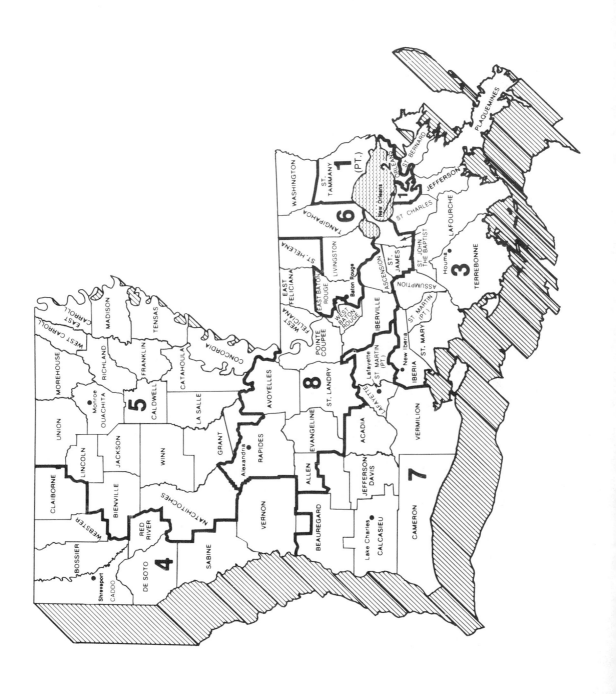

Louisiana

Population and growth

1980 population	4,205,900
1989 population estimate	4,382,000
(20th in the nation)	
Percent change 1980-1989	+4%

U.S. Congress

Senate 2 D
House 4 D, 4 R

State legislature

Senate 33 D, 6 R
House 86 D, 18 R, 1 Ind.
Governor Buddy Roemer, D

With no state-level elections until fall 1991 in Louisiana, the stage is set for a congressional redistricting process dominated by Democrats—albeit, for the most part, conservative ones. The Democrats, who have majorities of 33-6 in the Senate and 86-18-1 in the House, will draw the remap. Their final redistricting plan will then be sent to Democratic governor Buddy Roemer.

Although its late-1980s' population stagnation, brought on by the travails of its energy-based economy, has led to some speculation that Louisiana might lose a seat, most political demographers expect the state to hold its current eight. However, the Democratic control of the process will not be without consequence. It may provide some protection for Democrats Lindy (Mrs. Hale) Boggs and Jerry Huckaby, whose districts are likely to have to absorb some residents of nearby Republican-held districts.

Rearranging the New Orleans-based 2d District will be the most difficult chore for the legislators. The oil slump and the decline of some of New Orleans's inner-city communities caused a slight population loss in the 2d through 1986, even as the neighboring 1st, a conservative, suburban district held by Republican Bob Livingston, grew by more than 10 percent. Although the 2d is also bordered by Democrat W. J. "Billy" Tauzin's 3d District (up by 6 percent), it may have to pick up some territory from the 1st.

However, any reshaping of the 2d will have to be performed delicately, to avoid running afoul of black residents, who are about three-fifths of the district population. Protests by black activists in the early 1980s resulted in the voiding of Louisiana's initial district map, which split New Orleans's minority-group population between the 1st and the 2d districts. With black activists awaiting the retirement of Boggs (who is in her seventies), any remap that dilutes the 2d's black majority is certain to end up in court.

The other district facing an adjustment is Huckaby's 5th (northeast Louisiana), which is surrounded by the faster-growing 4th and 8th, held by junior Republicans Jim McCrery and Clyde C. Holloway.

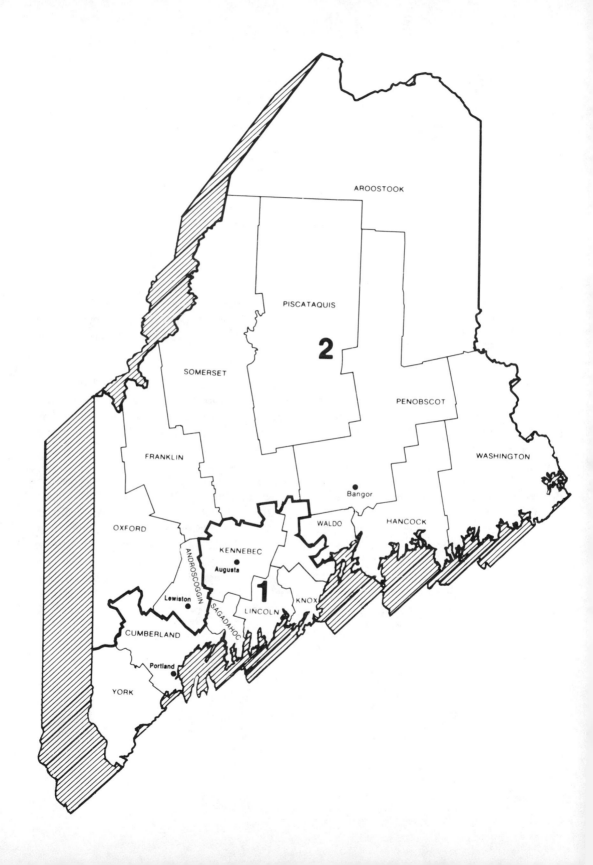

AROOSTOOK

PISCATAQUIS

2

SOMERSET

PENOBSCOT

FRANKLIN

WASHINGTON

Bangor

WALDO

HANCOCK

OXFORD

KENNEBEC

ANDROSCOGGIN

Augusta

1

KNOX

Lewiston

SAGADAHOC

LINCOLN

CUMBERLAND

Portland

YORK

Maine

Population and growth

1980 population	1,124,660
1989 population estimate	1,222,000
(38th in the nation)	
Percent change 1980-1989	+9%

U.S. Congress

Senate	1 D, 1 R
House	1 D, 1 R

State legislature

Senate	20 D, 15 R
House	98 D, 53 R
Governor	John R. McKernan, Jr., R

Since Maine slipped to two House seats in the 1960 census, redistricting has not been a matter of great urgency. The Legislature did not get around to its last remap until 1983, when it shifted 18,000 residents from the 1st District to the 2d.

The faster growth of the Portland-based 1st District over the more rural 2d during the 1980s will require another slight alteration in the map after 1990. In fact, the 1986 Census Bureau estimates showed the 1st with 36,400 more people than the 2d, a difference that, if it holds up, would require another transfer of about 18,000.

The 1990 gubernatorial election could weigh heavily on the next redistricting. Democratic representative Joseph E. Brennan, who served as governor from 1979 to 1987, is attempting to regain his former office. He is giving up his 1st District House seat to challenge his successor, Republican governor John R. McKernan, Jr. McKernan is currently the only one standing in the way of complete Democratic control of redistricting. Democrats hold both houses of the Legislature, with majorities of 20-15 in the Senate (all seats are up in 1990) and 98-53 in the House (including a ten-seat pickup in 1988).

Although the slight population differential presages minor changes, no matter who runs the remap, the outcome of the 1st District contest to succeed Brennan may have a bearing on how the job is accomplished. Since the 1st will have to lose some territory, a Democratic successor would likely offer up some rural turf, which should be readily acceptable to 2d District Republican representative Olympia J. Snowe. But a freshman Republican might try to convince the popular Snowe, a moderate who regularly wins by big margins, to accept some more urban and Democratic-leaning precincts.

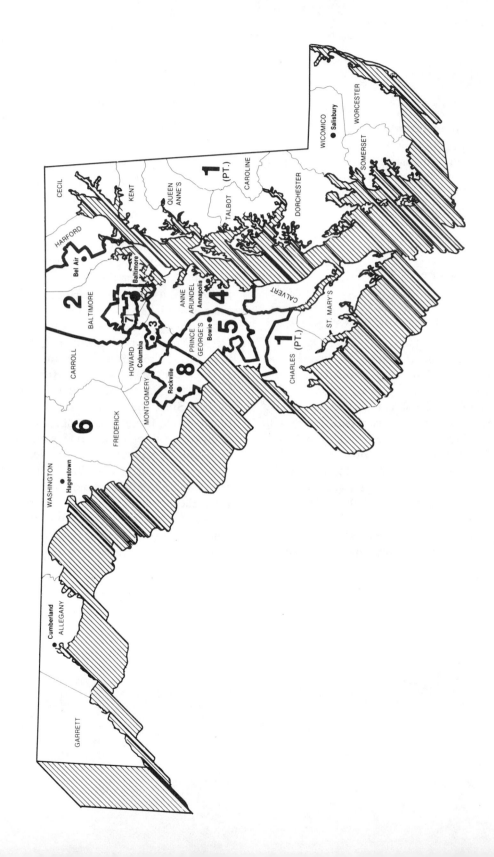

Maryland

Population and growth

1980 population	4,216,975
1989 population estimate	4,694,000
(19th in the nation)	
Percent change 1980-1989	+11%

U.S. Congress

Senate 2 D
House 6 D, 2 R

State legislature

Senate 40 D, 7 R
House 125 D, 16 R
Governor William Donald Schaefer, D

Despite the continued expansion of its suburban and exurban areas near Washington, D.C., and Baltimore, Maryland's overall growth rate of 11 percent through 1989 does not appear enough to earn it an additional House seat. Still, there are some fairly extreme population variations between the existing eight districts that will require adjustment.

The 8th District, covering most of Montgomery County in the Washington suburbs, grew by 15 percent from 1980 to 1986, according to the Census Bureau, and the 1st, 4th, and 6th districts increased their populations by 9 percent or more. But the 7th, a majority-black district based in inner-city Baltimore, lost 4 percent of its residents, and the 2d, the 3d, and the 5th all grew slowly.

If anyone benefits from adjusting these district lines, it will be the Democrats, who hold 88 percent of the seats in the Legisla-

ture, with majorities of 40-7 in the Senate (all seats are up in 1990) and 125-16 in the House. Democratic governor William Donald Schaefer, Maryland's dominant political figure, appears to have a lock on reelection in 1990, and Democrats have a 6-2 edge in the U.S. House delegation.

But Democrats will have some tough balancing acts to contend with in redistricting. The legislators, for example, will have to expand the 7th, held by black Democrat Kweisi Mfume, without seriously diluting the district's black majority; they will also have to take care of the interests of the Democrats whose districts surround the 7th, Benjamin L. Cardin (3d) and Beverly B. Byron (6th).

The legislators also have to take into account a black constituency in the Washington suburbs of Prince George's and Montgomery counties that has greatly increased its numbers and clout in the Democratic party. There was speculation last spring that black legislative leaders were planning to call for a majority-black House district to be created in that area in the next redistricting. Any significant change in the 5th could cause trouble for House Democratic Caucus Chairman Steny H. Hoyer; his district adjoins that of popular 8th District representative Constance A. Morella, a liberal Republican.

Following the initial local newspaper reports on the rumors, the chairman of the Legislature's black caucus denied that such a plan was in the works. But the story resurfaced in November 1989 in the *Washington Post,* spurring Morella to make an early statement against "infringement from other areas" on the 8th.

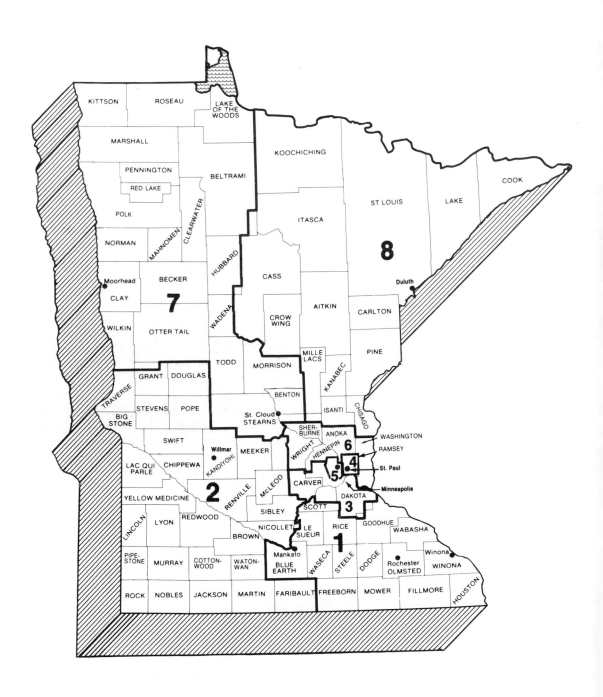

Minnesota

Population and growth

1980 population	4,075,970
1989 population estimate	4,353,000
(21st in the nation)	
Percent change 1980-1989	+7%

U.S. Congress

Senate 2 R
House 5 D, 3 R

State legislature

Senate 44 D, 23 R
House 80 D, 54 R
Governor Rudy Perpich, D

Minnesota has turned up on at least one long list of states that could potentially lose a seat, based on late-decade census estimates. But it is still seen as likely that Minnesota will be able hang on to all eight of its districts. Wide population variations have developed in the Minneapolis-St. Paul area, however, that will require correcting. Urban population growth has been rather stagnant, with the 5th District (Minneapolis) declining by 3 percent from 1980 to 1986 and the 4th (St. Paul) increasing by a similar percentage. These districts will have to expand somewhat into the rapidly growing suburbs for the 1990s.

Democratic governor Rudy Perpich is far from a sure bet for reelection in 1990, but Democratic majorities in both houses of the Legislature are solid: 44-23 in the Senate (all seats are up in 1990) and 80-54 in the House. So U.S. House boundaries can probably be adjusted without damaging Democratic incumbents Martin Olav Sabo (5th) and Bruce F. Vento (4th). These districts may be extended to the north, absorbing some of the excess population in the 6th District (up by 15 percent through 1986), which elected Democratic representative Gerry Sikorski and which supported Democrat Michael S. Dukakis for president in 1988.

The urban seats could also reach somewhat to the south, into the heavily Republican 3d, held by retiring GOP representative Bill Frenzel (also a 15 percent increase). But this district will likely have to donate some people to Republican Vin Weber's 2d, a rural, southwestern district that had a slight population decline through the mid-1980s (as well as to moderate Democrat Timothy J. Penny's slow-growth 1st District in the southeast).

The 7th (represented by Republican Arlan Stangeland) and the 8th (Democrat James L. Oberstar), which range from central Minnesota to the Canadian border, will also have to edge in closer to the Twin Cities. The 8th is estimated to have lost some population during the period, while the 7th grew by just 1 percent.

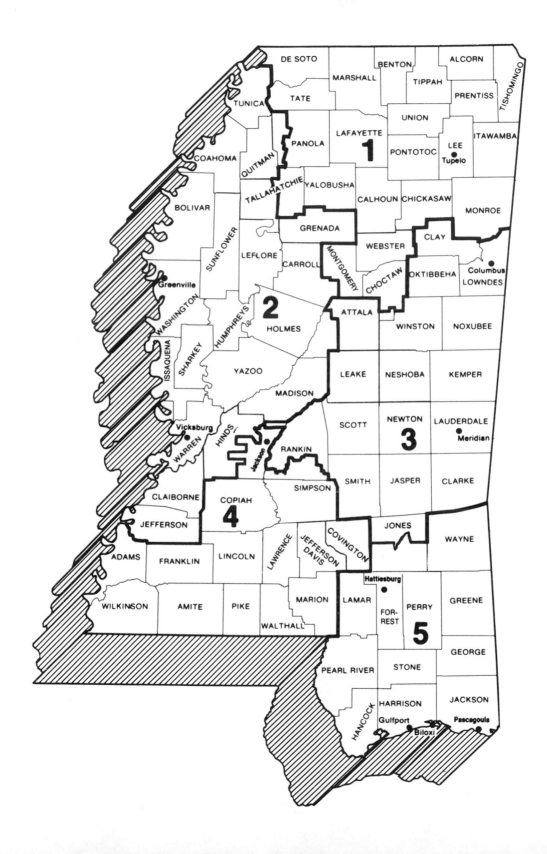

Mississippi

Population and growth

1980 population	2,520,638
1989 population estimate	2,621,000
(31st in the nation)	
Percent change 1980-1989	+4%

U.S. Congress

Senate	2 R
House	5 D

State legislature

Senate	43 D, 9 R
House	105 D, 17 R
Governor	Ray Mabus, D

Mississippi has no state elections until 1991, but Democratic control of redistricting was assured in any case. While the state's mainly conservative electorate has favored Republicans in national politics, its Democratic loyalties remain firm at the local level. Democrats have a 43-9 Senate majority (all seats are up in 1991) and a 105-17 House regime, despite an aggressive Republican effort to get conservative Democrats to switch parties (four state House Democrats did so in April 1990). The governor is Democrat Ray Mabus.

The state's five-district map needs only internal adjustments, but that task is not without some challenges. The 2d District, in the rural western area known as the Delta, saw a slight population drop from 1980 to 1986 and will have to pick up some territory in redistricting. The 2d is where Democrat

Mike Espy has made history in 1986, becoming the first black elected to the House from Mississippi since Reconstruction. In his first reelection campaign in 1988, Espy earned significant white support and a 65 percent victory.

But Espy's security depends on his base vote from the district's black majority (58 percent of the total); any redistricting plan that even unintentionally diluted that black vote would alarm Espy, black activists, and possibly the U.S. Justice Department.

During the last round of redistricting, Justice Department officials helped create the conditions for Espy's election. Acting on complaints from black activists and under the preclearance provisions of the Voting Rights Act, the Justice Department scuttled the initial remap, saying it divided black communities in a manner that precluded electing a black House member. Under another map that gave the 2d a slight black majority, white Republican Webb Franklin defeated a black candidate in 1982. In 1984 a federal court ordered a new remap; it created the current 2d, with its nearly 60 percent black majority. Franklin held on in 1984, but Espy unseated him in 1986.

An unexpected factor in redistricting is Democrat Gene Taylor, who in an October 1989 special election captured the previously Republican 5th District in southeast Mississippi. It is the constituency with the most population to spare; growth in its coastal region led to a population increase of more than 9 percent through 1986.

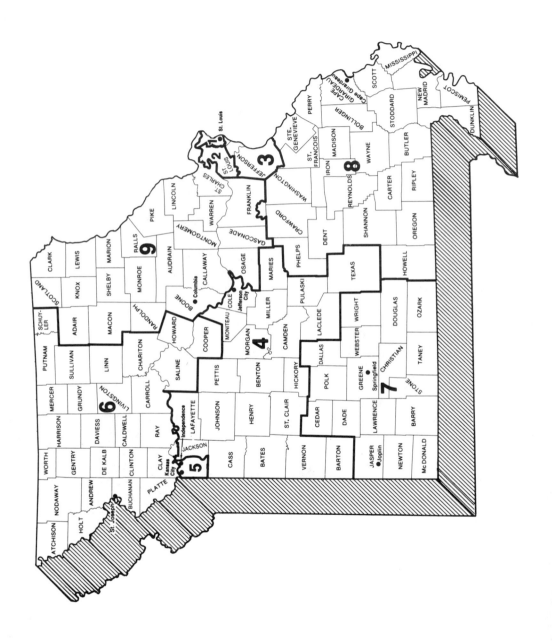

Missouri

Population and growth

1980 population	4,916,686
1989 population estimate	5,159,000
(15th in the nation)	
Percent change 1980-1989	+5%

U.S. Congress

Senate   2 R
House   5 D,   4 R

State legislature

Senate   23 D,   10 R,   1 Vacancy
House   104 D,   59 R
Governor John Ashcroft, R

Expected to hold at nine seats, Missouri should avoid the political bloodletting that ensued from its one-seat loss after the 1980 census. With the process then split between a Democrat-dominated Legislature and a Republican governor, redistricting efforts stalemated over whether to preserve the St. Louis-based 1st District represented by black Democrat William L. Clay; the district had lost 25 percent of its population in the 1970s. The remap fell to a federal district court, which drafted a plan favorable to Clay, then Missouri's only black House member.

Although it was extended into the northern suburbs, Clay's district maintained a slim black majority, helping him to win handsomely since. However, the ripple effect of saving Clay was felt in rural parts of the state: the dismemberment of freshman Republican Wendell Bailey's 8th District in south-central Missouri forced him into the 4th District, where he lost in 1982 to Democratic representative Ike Skelton.

The Missouri redistricters will have far less drastic changes to make after 1990. Clay's district lost only 3 percent of its population from 1980 to 1986. And though the 1st District's black majority will be at risk as it reaches farther into the suburban turf of the 3d District (held by Majority Leader Richard A. Gephardt) and the 2d (Republican Jack Buechner), Clay is now bolstered by nearly a quarter-century of House seniority.

Clay gained a black colleague in 1982 when Democrat Alan Wheat won Kansas City's 5th District. Wheat's district will also need some adjustments—it lost about 1 percent of its population through 1986—and may absorb some of the surplus in Skelton's 4th District, which has grown by more than 7 percent. Although picking up largely white suburban turf might cause Wheat some difficulty, he already has the distinction of being the black House member with the largest white constituency. He has won by landslides throughout his tenure, even though his district is only 23 percent black.

One other Missouri district must expand in the 1990s. The 8th, which includes the southeast Missouri protrusion known as the Bootheel, increased its population by just 1 percent through the mid-1980s. The surrounding districts—the 4th, the 7th, and the 9th—all had more robust growth.

As in the last round, both parties will have a say in remap deliberations. GOP governor John Ashcroft is already in place, having won a second four-year term in 1988. Democrats have firm holds on both houses of the Legislature, with majorities of 23-10 (with one vacancy) in the Senate (half the seats are up in 1990) and 104-59 in the House.

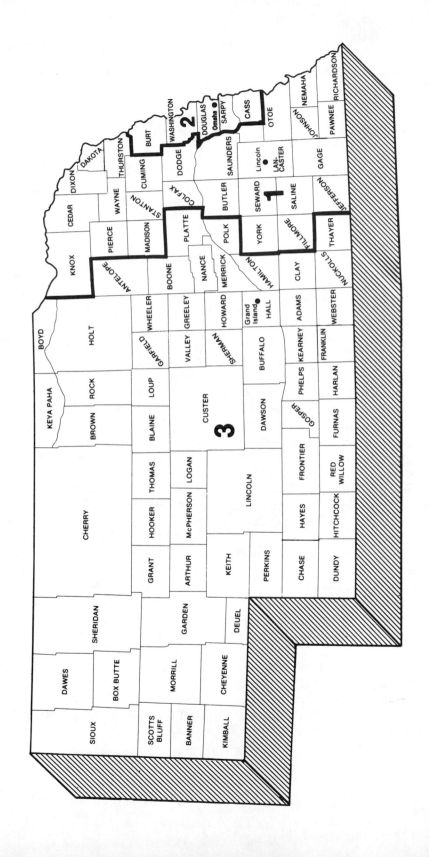

Nebraska

Population and growth

1980 population	1,569,825
1989 population estimate	1,611,000
(36th in the nation)	
Percent change 1980-1989	+3%

U.S. Congress

Senate   2 D
House   1 D,   2 R

State legislature

49 nonpartisan senators
in unicameral assembly
Governor Kay A. Orr, R

Nebraska's unique unicameral and technically nonpartisan Legislature (half the chamber is up in 1990) will have to make some minor adjustments to the state's three-district congressional map after the census.

Modest growth in the Omaha metropolitan area boosted the population of the 2d District (represented by freshman Democrat Peter Hoagland) by more than 5 percent. Growth was a bit slower in Republican Doug Bereuter's 1st District, which was up by just more than 1 percent, and retiring Republican representative Virginia Smith's sprawling agricultural 3d saw a slight decline.

Even the relatively small population difference of 35,000 between the largest and the smallest district in 1986 looms large compared with the situation after the 1980 census. Then, the three districts' populations were so balanced that the Republicans (who in reality dominate the forty-nine-seat Unicameral) tried to get by with no changes at all.

However, Democrats protested, and the Republicans drew up and enacted a plan that shifted six townships from the 2d District to the 1st and transferred rural Thayer County from the 1st to the 3d.

As in the last round of redistricting, Nebraska's governor is a Republican. But incumbent Kay A. Orr must stand for reelection in 1990.

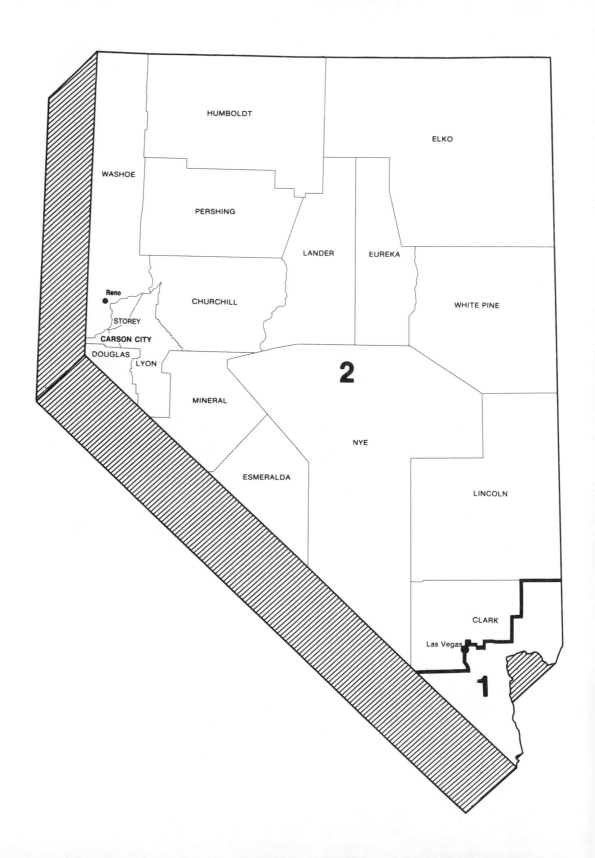

Nevada

Population and growth

1980 population	800,493
1989 population estimate	1,111,000
(41st in the nation)	
Percent change 1980-1989	+39%

U.S. Congress

Senate 2 D
House 1 D, 1 R

State legislature

Senate 8 D, 13 R
House 30 D, 12 R
Governor Bob Miller, D

Nevada's hypergrowth in the 1970s—its population increased by nearly 65 percent—earned the state a second House seat for the first time since its admission to the Union in 1864.

The state's population continued to soar from 1980 to 1989 (by an estimated 39 percent), carrying Nevada over the 1 million mark. But the increase will not take it beyond two seats for the 1990s.

With both of the state's House districts growing apace since the last census, it should be necessary to shift relatively few people between them: the 1986 Census Bureau estimates showed that the 1st, which takes in Las Vegas, had about 25,000 more people than the sprawling 2d, which includes Reno; the capital, Carson City; and lots of wide open spaces.

But the brief history of redistricting in Nevada is marked by partisan scrapping. During Nevada's first congressional remap in 1981, the Democratic majority in the Legislature tried to bisect Las Vegas so the state's largest city (and its only major font of moderate-to-liberal Democratic voters) would dominate both House districts. However, GOP governor Robert F. List threatened to veto any plan that was strongly oriented to the Democrats. Conservative Democrats from northern Nevada then lined up with the Legislature's Republicans, passing a coalition plan that concentrated metropolitan Las Vegas in the 1st.

Although the final, bipartisan plan worked to its desired effect—Democrats held the 1st through the 1980s, while Republican Barbara F. Vucanovich won the 2d in 1982 and has held it since—both parties will be fighting to ensure themselves a voice in the next round.

The Republicans are at the greatest risk. Although the GOP managed to reverse the traditional Democratic domination of the state Senate in 1986, they have just a 13-8 advantage (half the seats are up in 1990). In the Assembly, Democrats are firmly in control, 30-12. The governorship is also up in 1990; Democrat Bob Miller, who moved up from lieutenant governor after Democrat Richard H. Bryan's 1988 Senate election, is running for a first full term. The Republican party has not won the position since 1978.

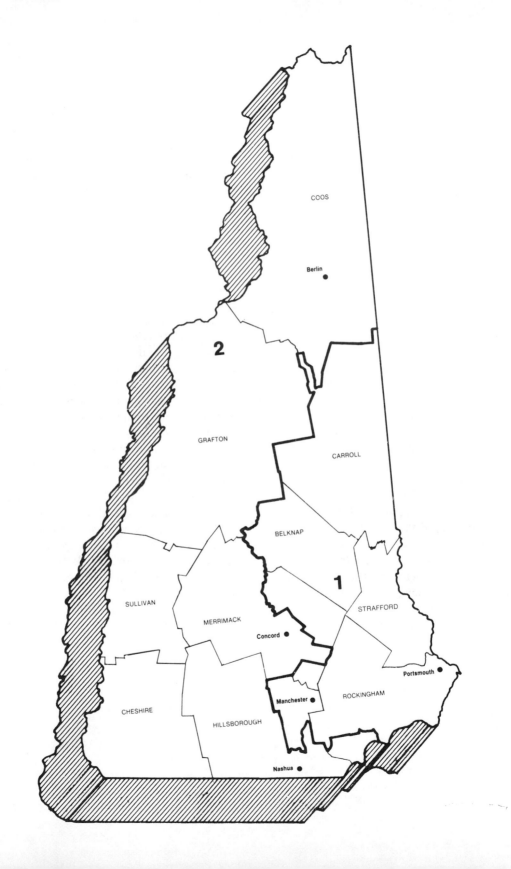

New Hampshire

Population and growth

1980 population	920,610
1989 population estimate	1,107,000
(40th in the nation)	
Percent change 1980-1989	+20%

U.S. Congress

Senate	2 R
House	2 R

State legislature

Senate	8 D, 16 R
House	119 D, 275 R, 1 Ind., 5 Vacancies
Governor	Judd Gregg, R

The postcensus prospects in New Hampshire are practically identical with those of a decade ago. The state's low-tax reputation and proximity to the Boston metropolitan area have extended the influx of new residents that began in the 1970s, enabling New Hampshire to remain the fastest-growing state (population up about 20 percent through 1989) in New England. Yet even with its population topping 1 million for the first time, New Hampshire will qualify for two House seats, and no more.

The 1986 Census Bureau estimates showed a 20,000-person difference between southeastern New Hampshire's 1st District (the part nearest Boston) and the 2d; if these figures hold up, about 10,000 residents will have to be transferred between the districts, just as in the last redistricting. And as in 1981, Republicans will likely control the redistricting process, virtually assuring that the population shift will do no violence to the Republican tendencies of both House districts.

The Legislature, which will originate the redistricting plan, is the most unusual in the nation. The 400-member House, a state-level extension of New Hampshire's traditional town meetings, is nearly twice the size of the nation's next-largest legislative chamber, the House in Pennsylvania, a state with nearly twelve times as many people. The constituent-to-member ratio in the New Hampshire House (about 2,500:1) is by far the smallest in the country. On the other hand, New Hampshire's twenty-four-member Senate is one of the smallest legislative bodies in the country.

The Republicans control both sides of New Hampshire's capitol. Even after a two-seat Democratic gain in 1988, the GOP holds a 16-8 advantage in the Senate. The Republicans' majority is even greater in the House, where they lead 275-119-1 (with 5 vacancies). Republican governor Judd Gregg will be up for a second two-year term in 1990.

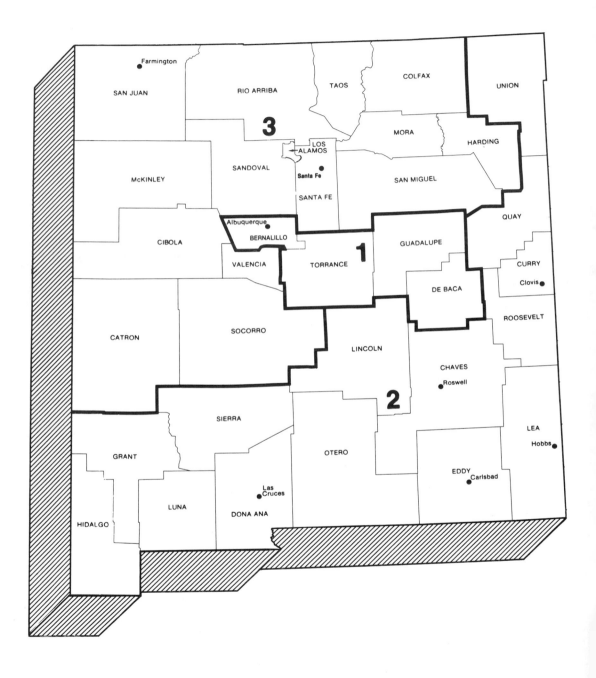

New Mexico

Population and growth

1980 population	1,302,894
1989 population estimate	1,528,000
(37th in the nation)	
Percent change 1980-1989	+17%

U.S. Congress

Senate   1 D,   1 R
House   1 D,   2 R

State legislature

Senate   25 D,   17 R
House   45 D,   25 R
Governor Garrey Carruthers, R

Joining the Sun Belt splurge, New Mexico experienced a population growth of 28 percent in the 1970s and moved up to three House seats. In the 1980s the state's growth, while still robust, was more moderate than that of the previous decade.

The state's remarkably balanced growth through the mid-1980s—population estimates show only an 8,000-person difference between the largest district (the 2d) and the smallest (the 1st)—points to a routine redistricting requiring few changes to the map.

Yet with the governorship open in 1990, Democrats will be taking a shot at control of the process. They have secure margins in both houses of the Legislature, with majorities of 25-17 in the Senate (no seats are up in 1990) and 45-25 in the House.

The last round of redistricting was actually more of an ideological than a partisan battle. An unusual coalition of liberal Democrats, Hispanic activists, and Republican U.S. House members blocked efforts by a bipartisan group of conservatives who sought to rearrange New Mexico's district map drastically.

The conservatives tried to create three conservative districts. Whereas the traditional map had divided the state into northern and southern districts, the conservative coalition's plan would have created an eastern and western configuration, bisecting the heavily Hispanic (and liberal) areas of northern New Mexico.

But Hispanics complained that the plan was an effort to thwart creating a Hispanic-oriented district in the north. They were assured of victory when the state's two GOP House members, Manuel Lujan, Jr., and Joe Skeen, objected to the conservatives' plan. Neither incumbent wanted a new map that would thrust thousands of unfamiliar constituents upon them.

The map that became law maintained Skeen's southern New Mexico base; created a central district, including Albuquerque, that Lujan (now secretary of the interior) held through his 1988 retirement; and established a northern district (Santa Fe), 60 percent Hispanic and American Indian, that has elected Hispanic Democrat Bill Richardson since 1982.

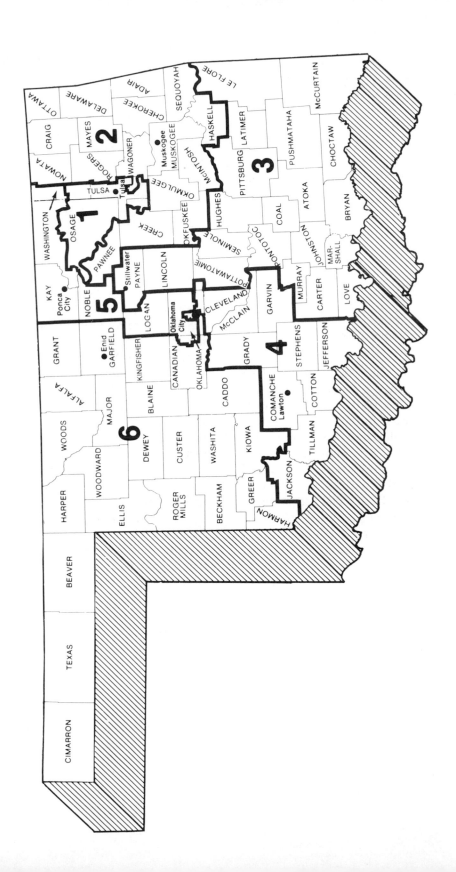

Oklahoma

Population and growth

1980 population	3,025,290
1989 population estimate	3,224,000
(27th in the nation)	
Percent change 1980-1989	+7%

U.S. Congress

Senate 1 D, 1 R
House 4 D, 2 R

State legislature

Senate 33 D, 15 R
House 69 D, 32 R
Governor Henry Bellmon, R

Oklahoma has had six U.S. House seats since the 1950s. With steady but unspectacular growth during the current decade, that is likely to remain unchanged after 1990.

All six districts gained population through the mid-1980s, although the rate was somewhat faster in the districts with urban concentrations, including the 1st, the 2d, the 4th, and the 5th, than in the mainly rural 3d and 6th.

Although district-to-district population disparities are not great, the 1990s redistricting may reverberate with the echoes of the partisan strife of the last round. Oklahoma Republicans decried the district map, enacted by a Democratic-controlled Legislature and signed by a Democratic governor in 1981, as a blatant attempt to grab five of the state's six House seats. The

GOP responded with an initiative drive to revoke the plan.

Republicans pointed out some of the map's artistic reaches. The 3d District, mainly in southeast Oklahoma, pointed a finger northward to take in Stillwater. Heavily Republican areas of Oklahoma City were placed in the 5th District, held by Mickey Edwards, then the state's only Republican member, but other parts of the city were put in the 4th and the 6th districts, represented then as now by Democrats Dave McCurdy and Glenn English. The tenuous Democratic edge in the Tulsa-based 1st was slightly bolstered by the transfer of a Republican section of that city to the 2d District, held by politically secure Democrat Mike Synar (in 1986, however, the 1st finally went Republican).

The GOP barely failed to convince a majority of voters that the plan was an egregious gerrymander. Their initiative was defeated in 1982 by a narrow 51 percent to 49 percent.

Democrats continue in firm control of the Legislature entering the final elections before redistricting. They have margins of 33-15 in the Senate (half the seats are up in 1990) and 69-32 in the House. This Democratic dominance raises the stakes in the 1990 gubernatorial election.

Republican Henry Bellmon, a former governor and U.S. senator, returned from retirement to capture the governorship in 1986, the first time his party had won the office since 1966. But Bellmon is retiring again, and the contest to succeed him is wide open.

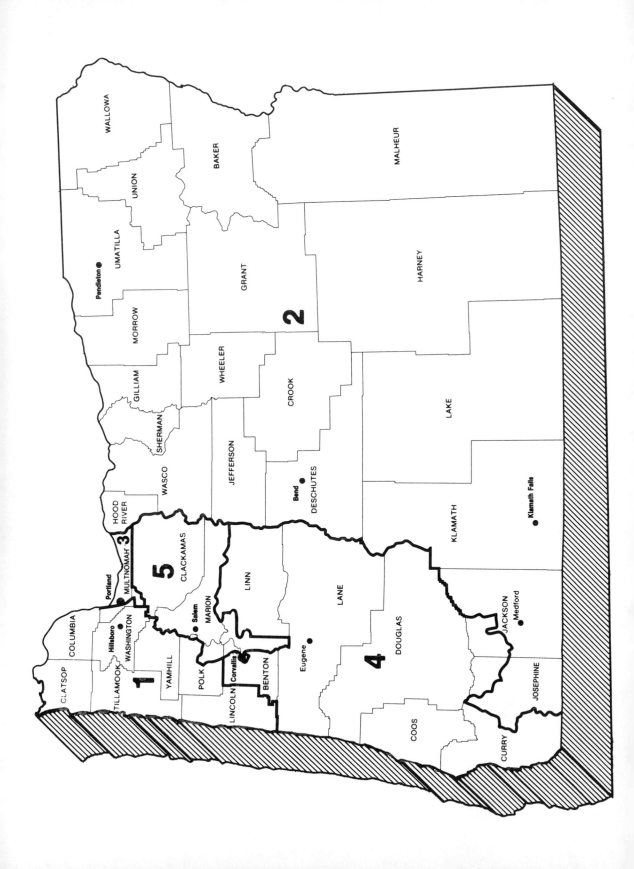

Oregon

Population and growth

1980 population	2,633,105
1989 population estimate	2,820,000
(30th in the nation)	
Percent change 1980-1989	+7%

U.S. Congress

Senate	2 R
House	3 D, 2 R

State legislature

Senate	19 D,	11 R
House	32 D,	28 R
Governor	Neil Goldschmidt, D	

An influx of more than a half-million residents during the 1970s earned Oregon a fifth House seat in the last reapportionment. But the migration has slowed considerably: Oregon's population was up less than 200,000 from 1980 to 1989, making it unlikely that the state will add a seat this time.

Oregon's House district map will still require some adjustments. Democrat Les AuCoin's 1st District, which includes the fast-growing Washington County suburbs west of Portland, showed a 7 percent growth rate in the 1986 Census Bureau survey. At the other extreme, flat growth in Portland was reflected in the population figures for Democrat Ron Wyden's 3d District. The heavily forested 4th District (Democrat Pe-ter A. DeFazio), dependent on a timber industry that has seen more downs than ups recently, actually lost people.

Oregon's last redistricting in 1981 was the least contentious among states that had to adjust for seat gains or losses. The Democrats, who controlled the Legislature, focused on bolstering Democratic advantages in the 1st and the 4th, which had become tenuous in the late 1970s. The new 5th District they created in the Willamette Valley (Salem) appeared so securely Republican that GOP representative Denny Smith abandoned the 2d District, which included much of his old eastern Oregon base, to run in it. The 5th turned out to be rather competitive, however; Smith won with 51 percent in 1982 and barely 50 percent in 1988. The 2d has stayed firmly Republican.

During the last round, Republicans had protection against Democratic redistricting abuse in GOP governor Victor Atiyeh. Going into the 1990 elections, Democrats control all the legs of the redistricting process, but have an iron grip on none of them.

Democratic governor Neil Goldschmidt unexpectedly announced in February 1990 that he would not stand for reelection, and the Republicans have a strong contender in state attorney general Dave Frohnmayer. The Democrats' margins in the state Legislature are rather narrow—19-11 in the Senate (half of which is up in 1990) and 32-28 in the House.

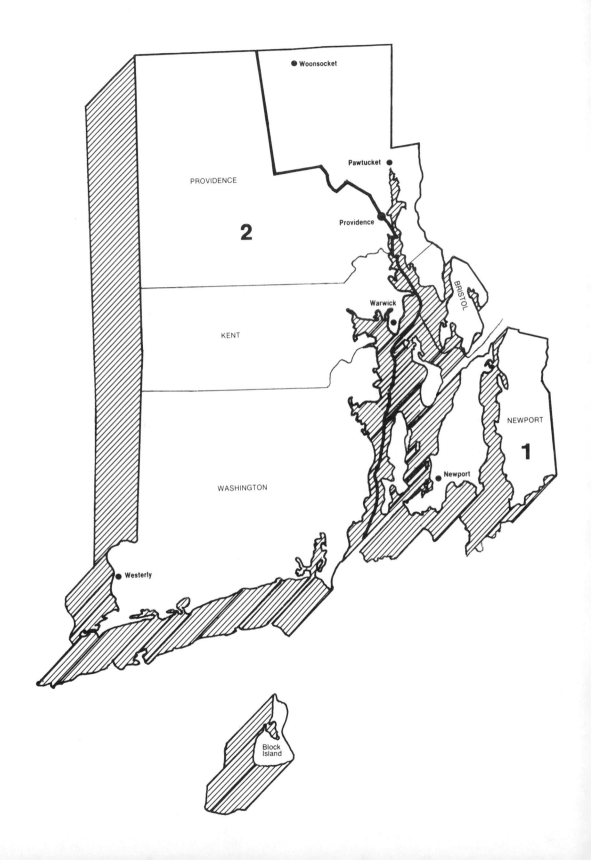

Woonsocket

PROVIDENCE

2

Pawtucket

Providence

Warwick

BRISTOL

KENT

NEWPORT

1

Newport

WASHINGTON

Westerly

Block Island

Rhode Island

Population and growth

1980 population	947,154
1989 population estimate	998,000
(43d in the nation)	
Percent change 1980-1989	+5%

U.S. Congress

Senate   1 D,   1 R
House   2 R

State legislature

Senate   41 D,   9 R
House   86 D,   14 R
Governor Edward DiPrete, R

With its population relatively level through the 1980s, Rhode Island will remain at two House seats—the state's representation in all but twenty-four years since Congress first convened two centuries ago. Slightly faster growth in the 2d District than in the 1st will require a minor adjustment of the district lines.

Although the Democrats' dominance in Rhode Island has faltered at statewide and federal levels, they retain a solid lock on the Legislature: 41-9 in the Senate (all seats are up in 1990) and 86-14 in the House. These Democrats' zeal for the post-1990 remap could depend on whether Republicans maintain their rare control of both U.S. House seats. GOP representative Claudine Schneider is giving up the 2d District for a 1990 Senate campaign against Democratic incumbent Claiborne Pell; 1st District Republican freshman Ronald K. Machtley, who upset veteran Democrat Fernand J. St Germain in 1988, will likely face a stiff challenge in 1990.

However, the Legislature has seldom shown a proclivity to make redistricting a partisan issue. And even if that changes, Republicans could well have a watchdog in the process: Republican governor Edward D. DiPrete, who is expected to seek a fourth two-year term in 1990. Should he win again, he would be the first GOP governor in place for Rhode Island redistricting since Norman S. Case in 1930.

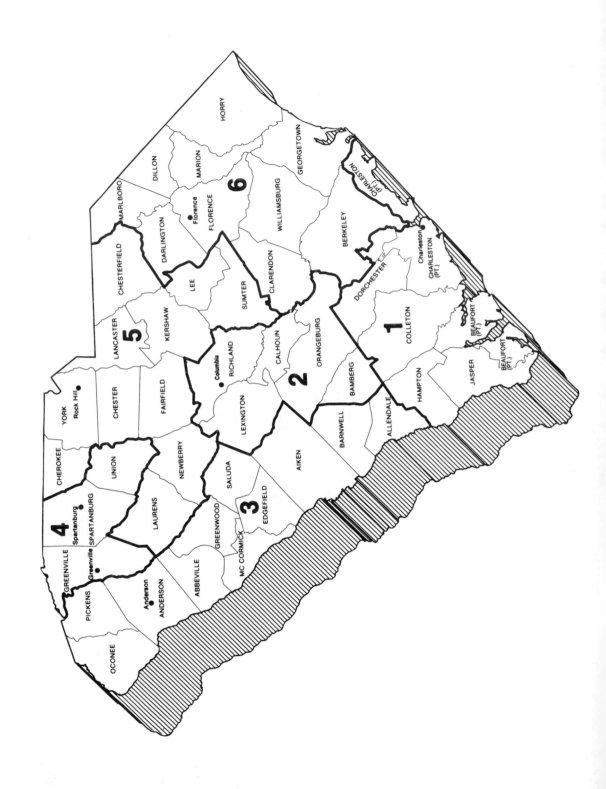

South Carolina

Population and growth

1980 population	3,121,820
1989 population estimate	3,512,000
(25th in the nation)	
Percent change 1980-1989	+12%

U.S. Congress

Senate 1 D, 1 R
House 4 D, 2 R

State legislature

Senate 35 D, 11 R
House 82 D, 42 R
Governor Carroll A. Campbell, Jr., R

South Carolina continued its steady growth through 1989, gaining about 400,000 residents, but the state is expected to hold at six House seats for the seventh straight decade. Census Bureau estimates showed that all six districts had population increases of 5 percent or more by the mid-1980s. As in the 1970s, the 1st District, which includes the Charleston area, led the way; its estimated growth through 1986 was 12 percent. (Whether the destruction Hurricane Hugo inflicted in September 1989 slowed Charleston's growth will not be known until the 1990 census results are tabulated.)

The 1st District's growth before the last redistricting was as great or greater, and efforts to redistribute its excess population of 40,000 tied the Legislature in knots. Several plans were scuttled, including one opposed by Democratic representative Butler Derrick that would have recast his 3d District to run all the way from the Blue Ridge Mountains in the north to the Atlantic Ocean in the south.

Even though the Legislature was then 87 percent Democratic, the redistricting battle ended in a stalemate that had to be resolved by a federal district court. The court-ordered plan made relatively minor changes, shifting only six of the state's forty-six counties, and it had little partisan impact.

The only district that changed party hands in the 1982 elections immediately after redistricting was the 6th, where Democrat Robin Tallon defeated GOP representative John L. Napier. (Napier had won in 1980 mainly because Democratic incumbent John W. Jenrette, Jr., had been convicted in the Abscam bribery case.)

The slight changes incorporated in the court remap did not please all South Carolinians. Black activists said the map should have been drawn to give blacks, who are 30 percent of the state's population, the majority in one district. But the Supreme Court upheld the lower court's plan in November 1983 without opinion.

Black leadership groups undoubtedly will pursue the same goal in the post-1990 process. Republicans also will raise their voices louder than ever. Republican governor Carroll A. Campbell, Jr., elected in 1986 as the state's second GOP governor this century, is a strong early favorite for reelection in 1990.

And while Democrats maintain substantial majorities in the Legislature (35-11 in the Senate and 82-42 in the House), Republicans have made headway through the decade. In the House, the GOP is encroaching for the first time on the Democrats' two-thirds, or "veto-proof," majority.

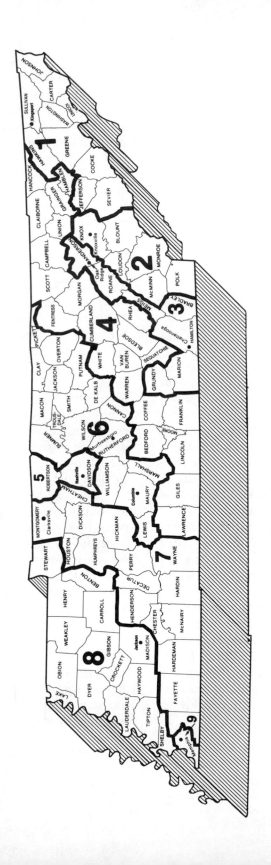

Tennessee

Population and growth

1980 population	4,591,120
1989 population estimate	4,940,000
(16th in the nation)	
Percent change 1980-1989	+8%

U.S. Congress

Senate 2 D
House 6 D, 3 R

State legislature

Senate 22 D, 11 R
House 59 D, 40 R
Governor Ned McWherter, D

Robust growth in the 1970s let Tennessee recoup a House seat it had lost in the previous reapportionment. But with its population growing more modestly in the 1980s, the Volunteer State is expected to hold at nine seats after the 1990 census.

Although both parties had a say in redistricting in 1981—Republican Lamar Alexander was governor, while the Democrats controlled the Legislature—redrawing the map to accommodate the new seat was accomplished with little partisan rancor. It was not done, however, without a degree of artfulness. The new 4th District, crafted from the leftovers of several surrounding districts, rambled in a series of steps from the northeast to the south-central parts of the state, encompassing twenty-three mainly rural, Democratic-oriented counties.

Some Republicans grumbled about an apparent gerrymander, but Alexander signed on to the plan, which protected the two veteran east Tennessee Republican incumbents, John J. Duncan and James H. Quillen; shaped a new-look 7th District that included much of the GOP turf that had helped elect Republican representative Robin L. Beard; and created a 4th District that Alexander thought could be competitive. He was right on most counts: Quillen and Duncan had no trouble holding their seats, and Republican Don Sundquist won the 7th. But Democrat Jim Cooper easily captured the 4th, which he has held since.

The Democrats appear likely to dominate the next remap. Democratic governor Ned McWherter, elected in 1986 to succeed Alexander, is strongly favored for reelection. Republican officials have said they will concentrate on winning at least one house of the Legislature. But this goal is a long shot: the Democrats have a 22-11 majority in the Senate (roughly half the seats are up in 1990) and a 59-40 margin in the House.

Even if the Democrats are in charge, it may be difficult for them to redraw the lines to penalize the GOP. While the fastest-growing House district in Tennessee through 1986, according to Census Bureau estimates, was Democrat Bart Gordon's 6th, the second-fastest was Sundquist's 7th. In addition, Democrats hold the slowest-developing districts, including the Chattanooga-based 3d and the majority-black, Memphis-based 9th.

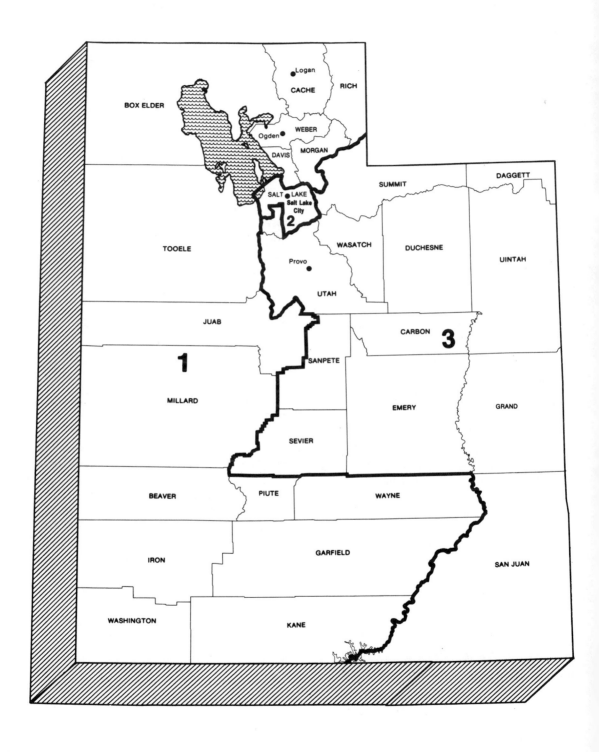

Utah

Population and growth

1980 population	1,461,037
1989 population estimate	1,707,000
(35th in the nation)	
Percent change 1980-1989	+17%

U.S. Congress

Senate 2 R
House 1 D, 2 R

State legislature

Senate 7 D, 22 R
House 27 D, 48 R
Governor Norman H. Bangerter, R

Utah, which gained a House seat in the last reapportionment, is expected to stay at three seats for the 1990s. The state's most recent population figures show an estimated 17 percent increase from 1980 to 1989, and imbalances in the growth rates of the three districts will require some alterations to the district map.

One prominent Utah Republican sent an early—and perhaps premature—signal that redistricting will be a partisan battle. Republican representative James V. Hansen caused a flap during the summer of 1989 when he circulated a plan that would have drastically reshaped the district map, to the probable disadvantage of Wayne Owens, the state's only Democratic House member.

Under the current map, Owens's 2d District is an urbanized region taking in much of Salt Lake County (including all of Salt Lake City). Hansen's plan would have taken most of Salt Lake County away from Owens, supplanting it with the rural, heavily Republican counties of eastern Utah. The 3d District (currently held by retiring Republican representative Howard

C. Nielson), which includes most of that eastern Utah territory, would have been shifted into Salt Lake City: the Democratic vote there would have been counterbalanced by the heavy Republican vote in and around Provo. Hansen's 1st District, the fastest growing in the state, would have to shed six rural counties to meet the ideal population but otherwise would remain much as it is today.

At one point, Hansen floated the idea that, because the population variation between the districts had grown so great during the 1980s, the Republican-dominated Legislature should redistrict immediately, without even waiting for the 1990 census figures. However, he retrenched after his suggested remap received a negative reception in the Utah media. (A Salt Lake City newspaper initially reported that the whole thing was a scheme perpetrated by the Republican National Committee, resulting in a tart letter of denial from the RNC and Hansen's acceptance of the role of "fall guy.")

The trial balloon perturbed Owens, who described it as a "blatant partisan gerrymander" and insisted that he should be left as "an urban congressman" after the next redistricting. The Democrat has good reason to be concerned about the partisan direction of the process: the Legislature has maintained its strongly Republican tone, with the GOP holding majorities of 22-7 in the Senate (roughly half the seats are up in 1990) and 48-27 in the House. And, unlike in 1981 when Democratic governor Scott M. Matheson held veto power over the plan, a Republican, Norman H. Bangerter, is in place for redistricting. He was elected in 1988 to a second four-year term.

The Utah Democratic party is backing a proposed voter initiative to establish a bipartisan commission for both congressional and legislative redistricting.

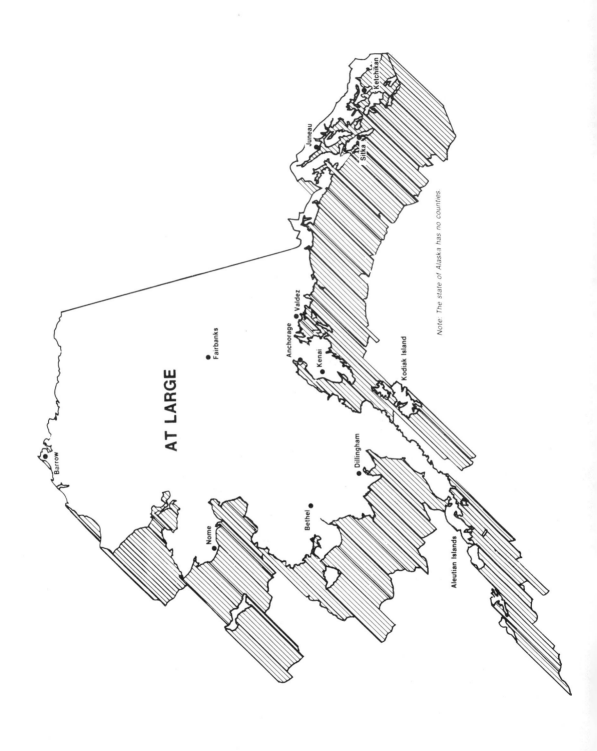

AT LARGE

Barrow

Fairbanks

Nome

Bethel

Dillingham

Anchorage
Valdez
Kenai

Kodiak Island

Juneau

Sitka

Ketchikan

Aleutian Islands

Note: The state of Alaska has no counties

9

At-Large States

The legislatures in the nation's six least populous states—Alaska, Delaware, North Dakota, South Dakota, Vermont, and Wyoming—need not worry with congressional redistricting: each has just one House member running "at large" (statewide), and none is expected to gain a seat after the 1990 census.

In fact, these states may be joined by Montana, which could drop from two seats to one, according to some population projections.

Following is a brief outline of the state legislative picture and other political forces in each single-member state.

Alaska

Population and growth

1980 population	401,851
1989 population estimate	527,000
(49th in the nation)	
Percent change 1980-1989	+31%

U.S. Congress

Senate	2 R
House	1 R

State legislature

Senate	8 D,	12 R
House	24 D,	16 R
Governor	Steve Cowper, D	

An estimated 31 percent gain in population through 1989 gave Alaska more than a half-million residents for the first time, but the state still ranks forty-ninth in population, ahead of only Wyoming. Control of the Legislature is split: Republicans hold a 12-8 majority in the state Senate (where half the seats are up in 1990), while Democrats maintain a 24-16 state House lead.

Democratic governor Steve Cowper has announced plans to retire at the end of his current term, setting the stage for a competitive gubernatorial campaign in 1990.

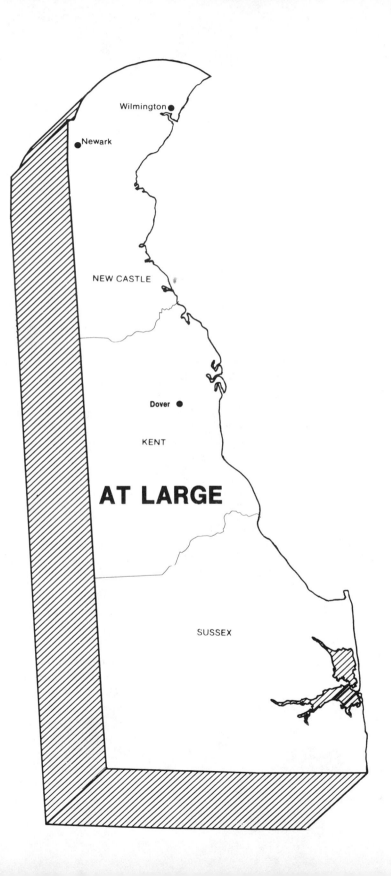

Wilmington ●

Newark ●

NEW CASTLE

Dover ●

KENT

AT LARGE

SUSSEX

Delaware

Population and growth

1980 population	594,338
1989 population estimate	673,000
(47th in the nation)	
Percent change 1980-1989	+13%

U.S. Congress

Senate 1 D, 1 R
House 1 D

State legislature

Senate 13 D, 8 R
House 18 D, 23 R
Governor Michael N. Castle, R

This state is an anomaly in the Boston-to-Washington megalopolis: outside of the industrial center of Wilmington in its northern reaches, Delaware remains rural and sparsely populated. The fifth least populous state in 1989 with about 673,000 residents (up 13 percent by the end of the 1980s), Delaware has had more than one House member only once in its history—during the 1810s.

The fairly even population split between urban Wilmington and rural southern Delaware contributes to a close partisan division in the Legislature. Democrats have a 13-8 state Senate majority (roughly half the seats are up in 1990), but Republicans lead 23-18 in the state House. GOP governor Michael N. Castle was reelected to a four-year term in 1988.

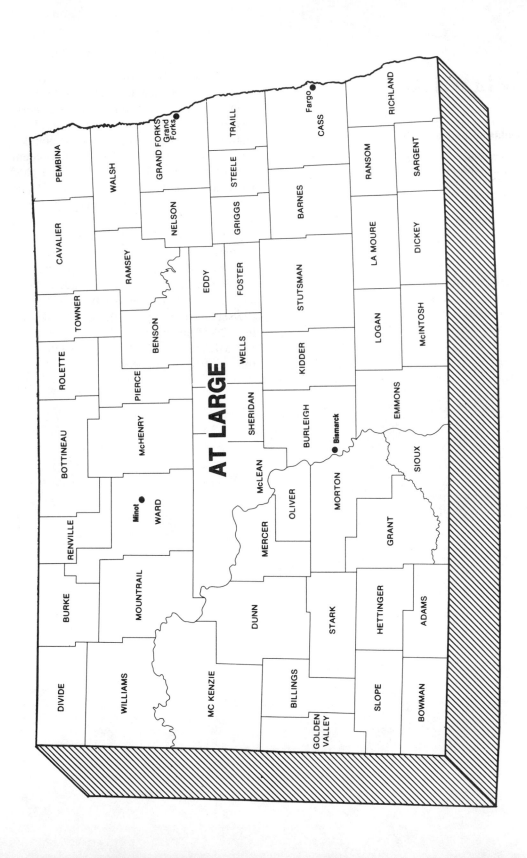

North Dakota

Population and growth

1980 population	652,717
1989 population estimate	660,000
(46th in the nation)	
Percent change 1980-1989	+1%

U.S. Congress

Senate 2 D
House 1 D

State legislature

Senate 32 D, 21 R
House 45 D, 61 R
Governor George Sinner, D

Suffering from the population stagnation typical of Farm Belt states, North Dakota lost its second House seat after the 1970 census and has no hope of regaining it in the 1990s. Its negligible growth rate (only 1 percent through 1989) has held North Dakota to 660,000 residents and dropped it behind Delaware on the population list.

The governor, George Sinner, is a Democrat, and his party extended its state Senate majority from 27-26 to 32-21 in 1988 (about half the Senate seats are up in 1990). But Republicans have a 61-45 majority in the state House.

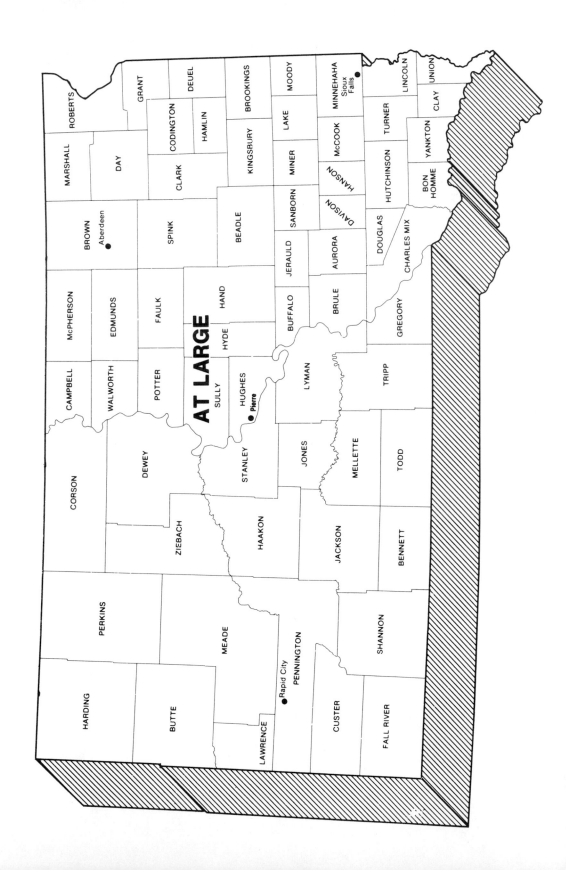

South Dakota

Population and growth

1980 population	690,768
1989 population estimate	715,000
(45th in the nation)	
Percent change 1980-1989	+4%

U.S. Congress

Senate   1 D,   1 R
House   1 D

State legislature

Senate   15 D,   20 R
House   24 D,   46 R
Governor George S. Mickelson, R

The last reapportionment was a sad one for South Dakota, which fell to one at-large district for the first time in its history.

The state's two House members faced off, with Democrat Tom Daschle (now a U.S. senator) besting Republican Clint Roberts. Its population has remained relatively level since (up 4 percent through 1989), so South Dakota will hold at one House seat.

The GOP is the leading party in state-level politics. Republican governor George S. Mickelson is up for reelection in 1990. The GOP controls the Legislature, with margins of 20-15 in the state Senate (all seats are up in 1990), and 46-24 in the state House.

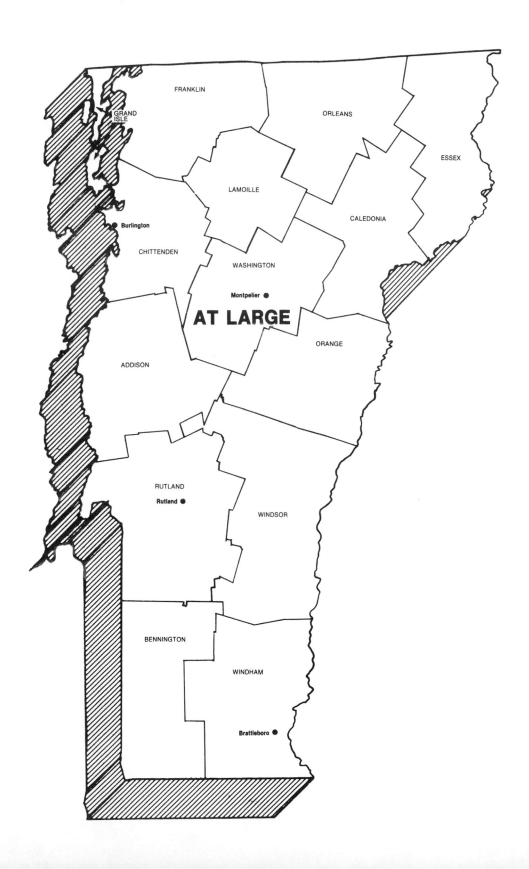

Vermont

Population and growth

1980 population	511,456
1989 population estimate	567,000
(48th in the nation)	
Percent change 1980-1989	+11%

U.S. Congress

Senate 1 D, 1 R
House 1 R

State legislature

Senate 16 D, 14 R
House 75 D, 75 R
Governor Madeleine M. Kunin, D

Once a rock-ribbed Republican bastion, pastoral Vermont has become one of the most politically competitive states, thanks to an influx of environmentalist and peace-movement liberals from the Northeast's urban corridor who have generally been friendly to Democratic candidates.

Vermont's senior senator is Democrat Patrick J. Leahy, and the state's Democratic governor, Madeleine M. Kunin, is in her third two-year term. The only Republicans to prosper statewide in recent years have been moderates such as James M. Jeffords, who was elected to the Senate in 1988 after seven terms in the House.

Vermont has hardly become a Democratic stronghold, however. Kunin, who has been assailed from both the right and left for some land-use and state spending decisions, announced in April 1990 that she would not seek a fourth term.

Former Republican governor Richard A. Snelling, who served four terms as governor before deciding not to run in 1984, has emerged as the frontrunner in the governor's race. The most likely Democratic candidate is Peter Welch, a former president pro tem of the state Senate, who ran unsuccessfully for the 1988 Democratic nomination to the U.S. House.

The partisan situation in the state Legislature is equally in flux. In the 1986 election, Democrats surged ahead in both houses. Republicans regained some ground in 1988, cutting the Democratic lead in the state Senate to 16-14 (all seats are up in 1990) and netting four state House seats to regain a majority, 76-74.

However, Democrat Ralph G. Wright was reelected House Speaker by a bipartisan coalition, highlighting the moderate-to-liberal tone that prevails in Vermont, even in the GOP. Kunin's selection of a Democrat in late 1989 to fill a vacancy in what had been a Republican-held seat evened the partisan score at seventy-five seats apiece.

Vermont has held at one U.S. House district since the reapportionment of 1930. With about 567,000 residents, it is the nation's third least-populous state.

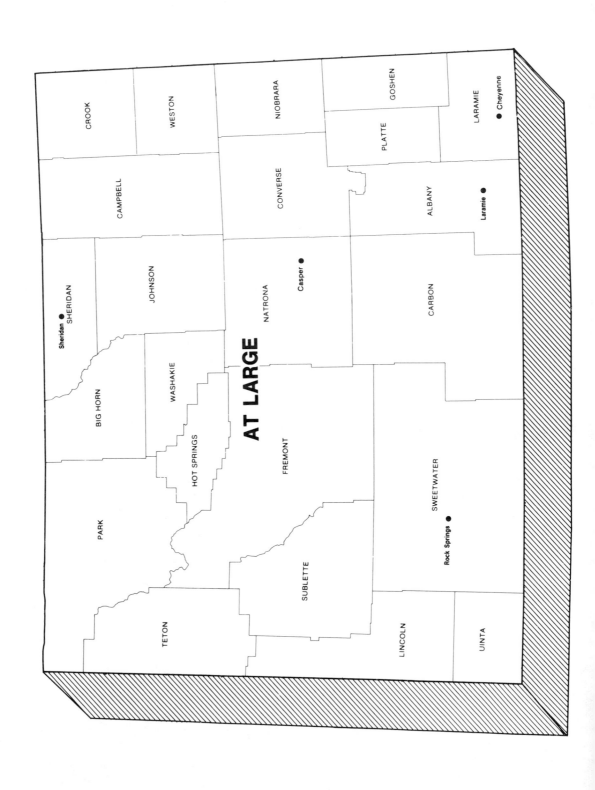

Wyoming

Population and growth

1980 population	469,557
1989 population estimate	475,000
(50th in the nation)	
Percent change 1980-1989	+1%

U.S. Congress

Senate 2 R
House 1 R

State legislature

Senate 11 D, 19 R
House 23 D, 41 R
Governor Mike Sullivan, D

Congressional redistricting has never been an issue in Wyoming, which has had one at-large House district since it became a state in 1890.

The least-populous state for much of its history, Wyoming escaped the cellar for a couple of decades after Alaska's admission to the Union in 1959. But the oil boom drew thousands of new residents to Alaska, knocking Wyoming, with its population of just 475,000, to the fiftieth rank.

Republicans continue their traditional dominance of the Wyoming Legislature, with majorities of 19-11 in the state Senate (half the seats are up in 1990) and 41-23 in the state House.

The governorship has provided a Democratic counterbalance since 1974 when Ed Herschler won the first of three terms. Herschler (who died in February 1990) was succeeded in 1986 by Democrat Mike Sullivan, who is up for reelection in 1990.

Index

DATE DUE